BRADFORD'S
OWN

DEREK A.J. LISTER

SUTTON PUBLISHING

Sutton Publishing Limited
Phoenix Mill · Thrupp · Stroud
Gloucestershire · GL5 2BU

First published 2004

British Library Cataloguing in Publication Data
A catalogue record for this book is available from the British Library.

ISBN 0-7509-3826-9

Typeset in 10.5/13.5 Sabon.
Typesetting and origination by
Sutton Publishing Limited.
Printed and bound in England by
J.H. Haynes & Co. Ltd, Sparkford.

This book is dedicated
to my late wife
Diana Mary Lister

1946–98

Contents

Foreword by Councillor John Stanley King,
Lord Mayor of Bradford 2000–1   v
Preface   vi
Bradford: An Introduction   vii

Foreword

This book is a long overdue and thoroughly deserved tribute to our fellow citizens who have distinguished themselves in many fields – art, entertainment, literature, music, sport, science, medicine and public service, to name only a few.

Some are well-known men and women of the present day, others have almost faded from memory, and few ever imagined that they would achieve fame.

We read with deep admiration of the acts of courage and bravery performed by ordinary men and women, as well as of the initiative shown by such people as 'the man who broke the bank at Monte Carlo', who provides a reminder that envy is one of the seven deadly sins!

I am glad that they have been commemorated in this way as a permanent reminder of people who by their talent, genius and sheer determination have contributed so outstandingly to the life and welfare of our great metropolitan city.

I thank Derek Lister for having invited me to write the foreword to this fascinating book which fills an important gap in the history of our area.

Councillor J.S. King, 2004
Lord Mayor of Bradford 2000–1

Preface

I was born and bred in Bradford and had, over the years, heard stories and rumours of individuals, past and present, who were born or lived in the city, or even adopted it as their home. Examples were Michael Rennie, Pat Paterson, Gertie Millar, Wilfrid Lawson and many others: but who were they?

You may find the odd reference to some of these people in an old biography or a snippet in a faded newspaper, but other than that most of these eminent sons and daughters of Bradford seem to have been forgotten. No plaque, statue or anniversary for them. In some cases they lie in unmarked, uncared-for graves, in unkempt cemeteries.

It became clear that there was nothing of real substance set down in any book to highlight the lives of many of these local people who contributed so much in their own spheres. I decided to rectify that, to bring together important figures from Bradford's past with important figures in its present, in a celebration of *Bradford's Own*.

There were many people to choose from and it has been difficult to include some and not others. With this admission I am sure that I shall be inundated with suggestions of those I have overlooked who should have been included. If so, then perhaps a second volume will be in order as more modern celebrities make their mark! In this book I have included people who come from the wider Metropolitan District of Bradford which covers Ilkley, Keighley, Shipley and Bingley.

My selection is the result of research over three years. I have endeavoured to include as much detail as space allows, especially with reference to the local connection. Overall, I want to create a record for future generations, for them to admire and to bring a glimpse of what has been, and is being, achieved by, in most cases, very ordinary people.

I was amazed and in some cases saddened to learn that many famous names from earlier times were let down by the city of their birth or adoption. Not that they expected gratitude for their achievements, but the city itself appeared *not* to be proud of its sons and daughters, many of whom were held in high esteem in politics, medicine, industry, music, theatre, films, sport, adventure and exploration. Other cities revere their past and present heroes and heroines, and some would indeed be proud to have just one of our Bradford's own. It is not too late for Bradford to make some amends to these people, perhaps by creating a city centre building in which to profile them. This would be a tourist attraction for the many visitors to Bradford and it would be a lasting way to express respect and gratitude to all our famous sons and daughters.

Bradford: An Introduction

Bradford is a surprising place. With almost half a million inhabitants it is the seventh largest city in the UK. Yet it has some of the most striking scenery in the country. To the north are the famous Ilkley and Rombalds Moors standing astride the wooded valleys of the Wharfe and Aire, rivers that flow from the Yorkshire Dales which border the area. Even more rugged are the high moorlands of the Pennines to the west, where the 'Wuthering Heights' draw visitors from across the world. To the south is the gently undulating country of Kirklees and the Calder valleys, and to the east are the lowlands of Leeds and the Vale of York. Equidistant from the ports of Hull to the east and Liverpool to the west, Bradford's strategic situation away from the flood plains of eastern England and sheltering in the lee of the Pennines, endowed with water and other natural resources, has meant the city has played an important part in the history of the UK, particularly during the industrial and multicultural revolutions of recent history.

Prehistoric remains indicate that Bradford ('broad ford') was settled early; many place names are of Celtic, Danish, and Viking origin; and Ilkley was a Roman fort. After the Norman Conquest, Bradford, like most of the north, was 'laid waste' by the Norman invaders. During the seventeenth-century Civil War, Bradford's support of Parliament in its fight with the Stuart kings resulted in a number of fierce battles, but this time a ghost (at Bolling Hall) saved Bradford from destruction! Wool and textile production date from the sixteenth century, but it was with the industrial revolution of the late eighteenth century – when fast-flowing local streams and then coal deposits could power looms, iron deposits provided machinery and the canals and railway transported raw materials and finished products – that Bradford, Keighley, Bingley and other townships developed into the textile centres that brought prosperity, fame, and rich cultural life to the area. In the 1880s Bradford was a centre of trade within the expanding British Empire, with numerous foreign consulates and immigrant workers. Only a few mills remain today, but many of the supporting engineering, chemical and commercial services have survived and developed. Today Bradford has a mixed economy with electronics, retailing, and tourism some of the largest employers.

This industrial heritage provides some of the most interesting and spectacular buildings to be seen today: Salt's Mill is a designated UNESCO World Heritage Centre and Lister's Mill, especially its chimney, is a wonder of the industrial world. The recently refurbished Wool Exchange and the warehouses of Little Germany are remarkable testaments to Bradford's importance in world trade; the Leeds–Liverpool Canal and its Five Rise Locks at Bingley is another wonder of the Industrial Revolution. The railway viaducts and tunnels testify to the skill of the pioneering Victorian engineers, as do the stylish Midland and Victoria hotels. Public buildings such as the Italianate City Hall and the Cartwright Hall Art

Gallery, public open spaces such as Peel Park (the venue of the annual multicultural Mela), Lister Park (named after one of Bradford's famous inventors) and the Industrial Museum are places to admire and treasure.

Bradford is more than just a busy city with an impressive industrial heritage. The cathedral and the many magnificent church buildings (now supplemented by mosques, temples and gurdwaras) throughout the region give testimony to the strength of the spiritual side of life; the Carnegie libraries at Keighley (England's oldest) and Ilkley, and the old college buildings in Bradford's student quarter demonstrate the drive for education and self-development; and the spa town of Ilkley of the drive for health. The delightful Edwardian Alhambra Theatre is a popular venue for plays, ballet, and pantomime; the Victorian St George's Hall, where Dickens once read, is now the venue for all manner of concerts; while the cobbled streets of Haworth which lead up to the Parsonage Museum are a magnet for thousands of visitors who pay homage to those world-famous authors, Charlotte, Emily and Anne Brontë. The Keighley and Worth Valley Railway and its regular steam-hauled trains, as well as being one of the country's premier preserved railways, also remind one of that delightful film *The Railway Children* – and Cottingley was the scene of those famous fairies!

The industrial revolution passed long ago, but Bradford continued to develop. Sunwin House and the Gaumont picture house are examples of pre-war Art Deco. The *Telegraph & Argus* building, the Magistrates' Court and new Crown Court buildings are strikingly successful examples of modern architecture. The Kirkgate Shopping Centre, John Street Market, the Transport Interchange, and the National Museum of Photography, Film & Television illustrate what can be achieved by refurbishing buildings. The latter has an IMAX screen, and one of only three Cinerama screens in the UK.

Perhaps nowhere mixes the old and the new as well as the massive Salt's Mills at Saltaire. Inside the enormous machine rooms is the largest exhibition of paintings by David Hockney in the world, exquisite furniture for sale, a bookshop and a diner. Other mill buildings are devoted to hi-tech electronic manufacturing. The surrounding streets, their appearance preserved from when philanthropist mill owner Sir Titus Salt built them, are now much sought-after prestige housing and shops, while the riverside Roberts Park leads to the historic Glen Railway and rocky Shipley Glen. (The fit and energetic make for Dick Hudson's hostelry on the moor, walk past the Apostles' Stone Circle, see the spectacular views of Ilkley from the Cow and Calf Rocks, and then, perhaps, the tea rooms, before getting one of the smart new electric trains back to the recently reopened Saltaire station.)

Bradford has always attracted folk from other regions and countries; successive influxes of people from Ireland, Eastern Europe, the Caribbean, East Africa, Southern Asia and the Balkans have today made the city their home. The resultant diversities of cultures and lifestyles have produced a vibrant and exciting multicultural mix: 'One landscape; many views', in the words of the city's City of Culture bid. If Bradford is conscious of its rich heritage, it is also conscious of pioneering a new one. Where Bradford leads; others may follow. Over six million visitors a year come to see this landscape and these views.

Mohammed Ajeeb CBE

Lord Mayor of Bradford 1985

In 1985 Mohammed Ajeeb became the Lord Mayor of Bradford, Britain's first Asian Lord Mayor – and the subject of huge media attention here and in the Indian subcontinent.

Mohammed was born in Mirpur, Pakistan, in 1938. Unlike the majority of children in the village, Mohammed attended the local school, then Dadyal High School, where he obtained a matriculation certificate. Aged fifteen he travelled to Karachi and did various manual jobs before securing a post with the Government Customs Department, simultaneously studying part-time for a BA degree at Karachi University.

In 1957 after graduating he came to Britain and settled in Nottingham. Here his work was varied, as a labourer, a shunter for British Rail, a bus conductor and a driver. Before moving to Bradford he was a housing officer with the District Community Relations Committee and founder member of many associations and services in Nottingham designed to overcome the problems encountered by immigrants.

In 1973 he was invited to take a post in Bradford as Deputy Director of Shelter Housing and Renewal Experiment (SHARE). In 1977 he was promoted to Director. His interest in politics began in 1974 when he first joined the Labour Party. An impressive rise through the hierarchy followed: he became a councillor in 1979, and this paved the way for his being made Lord Mayor in May 1985.

Mohammed Ajeeb dealt with his year in office with a quiet dignity. He succeeded in rallying all the people of Bradford whatever their colour. His work brought him the accolade of being acknowledged as one of the best Lord Mayors that Bradford has ever had.

He was a Labour councillor for many years, and rose to become Deputy Leader of the Labour Group in the years after it had won control of the council in 1990. However, his one disappointment was that he never became an MP, although he put up a good showing when he contested the constituency of Bradford North.

Mohammed Ajeeb is a remarkable man. His track record speaks for itself, and demonstrates his wide and varied experience. A Muslim of national and international repute, he is a man who has fought all his life for racial equality and social justice for all. He has the reassuring presence of an elder statesman, a quality that was recognised in the Queen's Birthday Honours List of June 2001 with the award of the CBE.

Private Eric Anderson VC
Victoria Cross Recipient, Second World War

Eric Anderson was born on 15 September 1915 in Fagley, the only son of George and Mary Anderson. He attended Thornbury Boys School and lived at Ashfield Place, Fagley. Before the Second World War he was a driver for a building and contracting firm in Idle and on Sundays sang in the choir at Eccleshill Parish Church.

When war was declared in 1939 Eric enlisted in the 5th East Yorkshire Regiment, sailing to the Middle East in 1941. By 1943 Pte Anderson, then twenty-seven, was a stretcher-bearer with 'A' Company, 5th Battalion East Yorkshire Regiment. Around this time, just before the Germans were chased out of North Africa, several ferocious battles took place in Tunisia. It was in one of these, at Wadi Akarit, that Eric Anderson was to achieve everlasting fame. On 6 April 1943, in the closing stages of the battle, Pte Anderson went out three times into no-man's-land to rescue wounded comrades, and had gone out a fourth time when he was shot and killed.

The citation in the *London Gazette* of 29 July 1943 recording the posthumous award of the Victoria Cross read: 'By his valour, complete disregard for his personal safety and courage under fire, he probably saved the life of three of his comrades, and his example was an inspiration to all who witnessed his gallant act.'

More specific were comments from his comrades that when he went out the fourth time, he was by now the only moving target left to shoot at, and he was still defying intense machine-gun and mortar fire. He was in the act of giving first aid when he was hit and mortally wounded.

His decoration was received by his widow from King George VI in October 1943 and the following year a memorial plaque was unveiled at Thornbury Boys School. In 1954, his widow, by then remarried, presented the Victoria Cross to his regiment in a ceremony at Beverley, then the Regimental Depot.

Pte Anderson's grave – the VC engraved upon its headstone – is in the War Cemetery in Sfax in Southern Tunisia.

Eric Anderson was the only Bradford man, the only member of the 5th East Yorkshires and the only stretcher-bearer in the Second World War to receive the Victoria Cross.

Sir Edward Appleton

Scientist and Nobel Prize Winner

Edward Victor Appleton became Britain's youngest Professor and Chief Scientist during the Second World War, when he was influential in guiding the development of radar.

The son of a working-class family, he was born in a back-to-back cottage in Maperton Road, Bradford Moor, in 1892. From Barkerend Elementary Boarding School he gained a rare scholarship to Hanson High School, where he captained both the football and cricket teams, and where in his first exam for physics he gained a mark of 100 per cent. He excelled at Hanson, and although he won a scholarship to Bradford Grammar School at sixteen, he appears not to have taken it up for the want of money. He won the Isaac Holden Scholarship, which was worth £150 over three years, and the money enabled him to study at Cambridge University, having first mastered Latin and Greek which were then compulsory entrance subjects.

When war came in 1914 he was already a scientist of great promise, but gave up his work to serve in the Bradford Pals (West Yorkshire Regiment). He later transferred to the Royal Engineers where he became a captain and an instructor in wireless signalling.

Returning to Cambridge he devoted himself to the new field of radio science, and in 1924 he proved the existence of the Heaviside Layer, part of the ionosphere. Radio waves could be bounced off this layer and thus travel long distances. During the Second World War, as the Chief Government Civilian Scientist, Appleton was especially influential in guiding the development of radar, Britain's early warning system, which detected incoming German aircraft and helped the RAF win the Battle of Britain.

In 1947 Sir Edward Appleton, who had been knighted in 1941, won the Nobel Prize for physics and also became a Bradford Freeman. In 1949 Appleton became Principal and Vice-Chancellor of Edinburgh University where he remained until his death at seventy-two in 1965.

Bob Appleyard

Yorkshire and England Cricketer

Tall, with an ideal cricketing physique, smooth bowling action and quiet, thoughtful manner, Bob Appleyard was a right-arm multi-purpose bowler, who took the cricket world by storm in 1951. Coming into the season virtually unknown, he headed the first-class averages.

He was born at the family home in Wibsey Bank, Bankfoot, on 27 June 1924. His first school was St Matthew's Primary, Bankfoot, and he later attended Priestman School. Leaving school in 1939, he was apprenticed in mechanical engineering at Hepworth & Grandage Engineering Company, Bradford, and Knowles & Company, Toller Lane. Towards the end of the war, although in a reserved occupation, he volunteered for aircrew in the RAF and was accepted, but he was later released because by this stage in the war casualties had been reduced and fewer men were needed. He volunteered again, this time as an engine room artificer in the Royal Navy. He was given the rank of petty officer and served in the Far East.

Back in civvy street and working in refrigeration engineering, he continued playing cricket for some of the best clubs in Yorkshire, namely Manningham Mills, Bowling Old Lane and Undercliffe, in the Bradford League. During this time he was beginning to make a name for himself as a fast bowler and came to the notice of Bill Bowes, the county bowling coach. Bowes was so impressed that he gave Bob trials with the Yorkshire Colts. He was so successful they made him a regular member of the team.

In 1950 he was given three matches in the first team but 1951 was his golden summer. He set a record for a player appearing in his first full season by taking 200 wickets at 14.14 runs each for Yorkshire, a truly great performance as he also headed the national bowling averages. The glory of his first season was shattered when Bob, struck down with tuberculosis, missed the next two seasons. After major surgery and eleven months in hospital, the Yorkshire Cricket Club sent him to Switzerland for a month's convalescence.

On his return to first-class cricket in 1954 he showed that he had lost none of his bowling powers by taking 141 wickets for the county. He also gained his first test cap playing against Pakistan, taking 7 wickets. That winter, 1954/55, Bob was selected for the tour to Australia, where he played in the last four Tests (England having lost the first one); three were won, the other drawn. Bob gave great support to the fast bowlers, Frank Tyson and Brian Statham in the Test Series by taking 11 wickets at 20.36 runs each. The series ended with the final Test Match drawn, and the series won by three to one for England to retain the Ashes.

The tour ended with two Test wins in New Zealand, England bowling out the Kiwis for 26 runs in their second innings of the second match at Auckland, the lowest score in a Test Match innings (still a test match record to date). Bob Appleyard took 4 wickets for 7 runs.

The summer of 1955 was a mixed one for Bob as he missed the latter half of the season through a shoulder injury, but he still took 73 wickets at an average of 11.54 each, finished top of the first class bowling averages, and played in a Test Match against South Africa. Returning in 1956, Bob captured 110 wickets for Yorkshire in a season that saw him make his final test appearance for England. Although affected by injury during the 1957 season, Bob still had 69 victims for the county. His last season for Yorkshire was 1958; he could only play nine matches. At the season's end the county awarded him a joint testimonial with Frank Lowson.

Taking into account the fact that he was a 'late starter' at twenty-six years old, had a serious illness and was troubled with injuries, it is a tribute to Bob Appleyard's determination and bowling skills that he took over 700 wickets in first-class cricket at only 15.48 runs each, and reached Test Match status. One can only imagine what heights and wickets-total this great bowler would have achieved had he started younger and enjoyed better health.

In the 1970s Bob became a Yorkshire committee member representing Bradford. He worked hard to help found a school for young players that eventually brought a cricket academy to Park Avenue. He was also involved in the Sir Leonard Hutton Foundation Scheme for young cricketers. In 1997 he was awarded an honorary doctorate by Bradford University.

Tasmin Archer

Singer-songwriter

Tasmin Archer became the first UK woman to have a solo number one hit in over a decade when 'Sleeping Satellite' topped the charts at the end of 1992. She was born on 3 August 1963 at St Luke's Hospital, Bradford, and her family lived at 90 Heath Terrace, off Leeds Road. She attended St Peter's Roman Catholic Infants School and then St George's RC Middle School. Later, when the family moved to Canterbury estate, she went to Grange Upper School on Haycliffe Lane, Little Horton.

She left school with several CSEs and her first job was as a sewing machine operator at S.R. Gent's. Feeling the need to improve herself she went on an introductory course at Bradford College, did a home study typing course, and then took the RSA examination and qualified. After a few temporary positions, she eventually became a clerk at Bradford Magistrates' Court.

From the age of five, her first love was music. She was influenced by her mother's records of Nat King Cole and the Irish tenor Josef Locke and knew from childhood that she just wanted to sing. It was while she was working as a clerk that she joined a group called Dignity as a backing vocalist. The lead guitarist would pick out harmonies for her on his guitar, helping her to build up quite a repertoire. Dignity had already been on the scene for some time and over the period Tasmin was with them they travelled away many times; sometimes she didn't return home until 6 a.m. and then had to leave at 7.30 for work.

Eventually she found work at Flexible Response, a Bradford studio run by Philip Edwards, where she cleaned and made the tea, as well as helping out with backing vocals. It was during this time that with the help of Philip Edwards, she met her future song-writing partners John Hughes (guitar) and John Beck (keyboard). For a time they worked together under the name The Archers.

After many returned tapes and disappointments, they were signed by EMI in 1990. The song 'Sleeping Satellite' had been in the band's repertoire for many years when they recorded it in 1992. On its release it reached number one. Archer won the Brit Award for best newcomer.

Still working with John Hughes, a solo album followed, *Bloom*, and a single, 'One More Good Night with the Boys'. In 1996, feeling she was becoming a commodity and not liking the business side of her music career, she stopped recording, but Archer and her partner John are still songwriting and still live in the area.

David Bairstow

Yorkshire and England Cricketer

David Leslie Bairstow fitted effortlessly into the best traditions of Yorkshire cricket, and was often the focal point of the Yorkshire team he served for two decades. Squat, broken-nosed, and forthright in language and opinions, he met all the requirements of the Yorkshire man who loved his sport and his pint of beer. His shock of red hair, which earned him the nickname 'Bluey', was entirely in keeping with his fiery character.

Born in Bradford in September 1951, David, from Bradford Moor, was educated at Hanson Grammar School, Barkerend Road. Aged fourteen, he was playing for Bradford Boys, and then turned out for a year with Laisterdyke, before moving to Undercliffe Cricket Club. At the same time he was also playing football and badminton and represented Bradford schools, which left him no time for study.

As a talented all-rounder he played a handful of games for Bradford City as a centre-forward, but cricket was his first love and he certainly made a big impression on his chosen sport. His debut came in 1970 when he was selected to play his first first-class match for Yorkshire against Gloucestershire at Park Avenue. Because of this he had to take his A-level exam at Hanson Grammar School by special arrangement at 6 a.m.

Bairstow went on to hold more catches behind the stumps than anyone else in the club's history, taking 903 wickets in first-class matches. His total number of dismissals reached 1,036. He was also a good hard-hitting middle-order batsman, which brought him 12,485 runs, putting him among the top thirty of the county's all-time scoring greats. David represented England four times at test level between 1979 and 1981, also playing 21 times in one-day internationals.

In 1987 the pressures of captaining, wicket-keeping and batting were beginning to take their toll, and his position as wicket-keeper was under threat from Richard Blakey. Bairstow was unhappy, but fought hard and forced his way back into the side, completing well over 1,000 dismissals before the final curtain came down on his career.

After finishing with Yorkshire he skippered his club side Undercliffe in the Bradford league for a couple of years, and became a cricket summariser for BBC Radio. David died in January 1998 aged forty-six.

Rodney Bewes

Actor

For twelve years *The Likely Lads* made Bingley-born Rodney Bewes one of TV's most highly paid stars. Forty years later the series is an icon of a golden age of comedy.

Rodney Bewes was born on 27 November 1939. The family lived at Longwood Avenue, near Bingley Grammar School. His father worked at the YEB showrooms in Forster Square, Bradford, as a clerk, and most of his relations had been mill workers. Rodney's early schooling was spasmodic; much of his childhood was spent in bed with asthma, reading Charles Dickens and building toy theatres out of shoeboxes.

At the age of twelve he read in his dad's *Daily Herald* that the BBC was looking for child actors. The enterprising Rodney despatched a letter, was auditioned, and soon found himself cast in several *Children's Hour* plays. At fourteen he moved to London to study at RADA's Preparatory School before graduating to RADA proper, from where he was expelled for his poor work rate – 'We think his talents would be better channelled into another profession'!

Putting aside his disappointment he won a role in John Schlesinger's superb *Billy Liar*, starring Tom Courtenay, which was mostly filmed in Bradford. Later Rodney auditioned for *The Likely Lads*, for the part of Bob Ferris.

The 'Likely Lads' made their first appearance in the 1963 *Christmas Night with the Stars*, introduced by Jack Warner. This taster introduced the audience to *The Likely Lads*. The combination of Rodney's enlightened and liberal Bob Ferris, and James Bolam's reactionary and straight-talking Terry Collier, was an instant hit. Filmed between 1964 and 1966, twenty episodes were made of the story of two Newcastle lads trying to get on in life.

Rodney then wrote and produced *The Basil Brush Show*, and was also the fox's first co-presenter. In 1968 he wrote, produced and starred in the sitcom *Dear Mother, Love Albert*. The show was a hit and became a mainstay of Thames TV. It was in the top ten ratings between 1968 and 1971.

The 'boys' were still hard up by the time *Whatever Happened to the Likely Lads?* surfaced in January 1973 (in colour). The series ended two years later. There was also a well-received radio adaptation.

Rodney's acting career of fifty years has also included *My Friend Dennis*, *Spender*, and films such as *Spring and Port Wine* with James Mason. He has played many roles in theatre and most recently toured with his successful one-man show, *Three Men in a Boat*.

The Rt Revd Alfred W.F. Blunt DD
Bishop of Bradford

The Bradford Diocesan Conference is an unlikely venue for a sensational news story, but the Bradford *Telegraph & Argus* report of that event on Tuesday 1 December 1936 triggered a chain of events that led to one of the most dramatic events of the twentieth century – the abdication. It was the then Bishop of Bradford, Dr Alfred Blunt, who made a speech which prompted King Edward VIII to step down from the throne because of his love for Mrs Wallis Simpson.

Alfred Walter Frank Blunt was born on 24 September 1879. In 1907 he was ordained into the priesthood. He became Bishop of Bradford in 1931.

During his early days in Bradford, living at Horton Old Hall, he gained widespread approval for his personal kindliness; in fact, he overworked himself with lamentable consequences and fell victim to four nervous breakdowns. His sermons and addresses to his diocese were renowned for their provocative language, and this was to the fore at the diocesan conference in 1936.

The public was unaware of the king's affair before the *Telegraph & Argus* devoted seven columns to 'The Bishop of Bradford's Reference to the King's "Need for Grace"'. It quoted Dr Blunt's remarks that the king should give more positive signs of his awareness to his duty.

Knowing the potential impact of the bishop's words, the newpaper's editor, O.B. Stokes, decided to use the story and it was his reporter, Charles Leach, who telephoned the speech to the Press Association and Extel news agencies the same afternoon. The bishop's criticisms were taken up by Fleet Street and the storm that led to the abdication ten days later was let loose.

It was ironic that Bishop Blunt had not even heard of Mrs Simpson when he wrote the speech some two months previously. He said the reason for his choice of words was that he thought it unfortunate that there was an impression that the king did not care twopence about religion. Between writing the speech and actually delivering it, he had been shown some newspaper cuttings about the king and Mrs Simpson by a fellow bishop, but had decided to go ahead with the speech because it had nothing to do with the lady.

Blunt was a most unselfish and devoted bishop, and it is unlucky that he is most remembered for this incident. In August 1955 and in failing health he resigned his bishopric. He died on 2 June 1957 aged seventy-eight, and is buried with his wife at Calverley Parish Church.

Dickie Bond

Bradford City and England Footballer

Certainly one of Bradford City's greatest stars, England international Dickie Bond was regarded as the best outside-right in Britain in the early 1900s. 'The firebrand with the face of a cherub', they used to call him in Bradford City's great days. But he could do more to disturb the peace and harmony of a football match than a gang of suffragettes.

Born Richard Bond in 1883 at Garstang, near Fleetwood, he began playing football with the Royal Artillery when serving as a Territorial. It was in 1902 that he first signed as a professional for Preston. He gained a Second Division championship medal in 1904 and two years later was a regular member of their team which finished league championship runners up. He was later selected to play for England.

Believing that a knee injury had left him with a permanent disability, Preston North End sold him to Bradford City at a reduced fee in May 1909. Dickie came to Bradford and became the greatest figure the city side had ever known. He was the idol of the Valley Parade masses for thirteen years. He was an outside-right who always took the shortest route to goal and has not, perhaps, been surpassed by any player Bradford City has known since.

In the 1910 season Bond played in all three home internationals for England, but perhaps his biggest disappointment was missing the 1911 FA Cup Bradford City v. Newcastle match because he had been suspended for using 'improper language' directed at the crowd when playing against Arsenal.

During the First World War he joined the 'Bradford Pals' 16th Battalion West Yorkshire Regiment, but in July 1916 he was taken prisoner by the Germans. It was said that the Germans hoisted a sign over the front line – 'We have captured Dickie Bond'. Whether this was a reassurance from the enemy that he was safe or a boast was not too clear, but the City fans were truly relieved to see their hero was unharmed and fit when he returned to the football league in 1919.

Bond received a record benefit at City of £700 after a match against Newcastle in February 1920, and was appointed club captain. Following City's relegation in 1922, he signed for Blackburn and in 1923 moved to Lancaster Town for a season. His league career brought 96 goals in 473 appearances despite losing four seasons to the war.

After retiring from football he became a publican in Preston, and died there on 25 April 1955 aged seventy-one.

John Braine

Novelist

John Gerald Braine is best known for the novel *Room at the Top*. This gritty story set against the background of 1950s Bradford and Bingley, chronicles the swift rise of the ruthlessly ambitious Joe Lampton from the petty bureaucracy of local government into the unfamiliar world of inherited wealth, fast cars and glamorous women. Memorably filmed with Laurence Harvey, Simone Signoret, Donald Wolfit and Heather Sears in the lead roles, it won an Oscar for Best Screenplay.

Born at 1 Sedgefield Terrace, off Westgate, Bradford, on 13 April 1922, John Braine went to Thackley Board School and St Bede's at Heaton. His first job was as a lab technician at Bradford College. This was followed by employment in Christopher Pratt's furniture store, as a progress chaser at Hepworth & Grandage, helping out in Mickey White's second-hand bookstore in Westgate, and as an assistant in the old Bingley Library. (His mother worked in the old Central Library in Darley Street; his father as a Superintendent at Esholt Sewage Works.) War service in the Royal Navy was spent mostly at Grassington Sanatorium, ill with tuberculosis. Here he started to write. After qualifying as a librarian he became Senior Assistant at Bingley Library on Main Street.

In 1951 he gave up his job, moved to London to be a writer and nearly starved. Library posts in Northumberland and Darton (Wakefield) followed another 18 months at Grassington Sanatorium. In 1957 the publication of *Room at the Top* made John Braine famous. Quitting libraries to write full-time again, he returned to live for a while in Park Road, Bingley. Twelve novels followed, but only *Life at the Top* approached best-seller status. However, his two non-fiction books, *How to Write a Novel* and a biography of J.B. Priestley, are still highly regarded.

Braine's early frustration with, and contempt for, the drab postwar establishment was shared by other writers such as John Osborne, Kingsley Amis, Alan Sillitoe and John Wain – 'The Angry Young Men'. Braine's early radicalism and admiration for the Soviet Union turned sour and he became increasingly cynical and reactionary. He lost the support of the predominantly left-wing London literati and became isolated (a period chronicled in his novel *Queen of a Distant Country*). He retained family connections and friends in the Bradford area over many years.

John Braine died on 28 October 1986 aged sixty-four in Hampstead, London. He was cremated at Bingley Cemetery and his ashes are buried there.

Jim Breaks

International Professional Wrestler

They say that Yorkshiremen are tenacious. If that's true then Jim Breaks is a true son of Yorkshire. With 10st 11lb all packed neatly into a 5ft 4in frame, his schoolboyish looks completely belied the skill and ring-knowledge of the former mill boy.

Jim was born 1937 in Bradford. As a schoolboy at Woodroyd School, he played football and excelled as a diver, representing Bradford in swimming galas. Boxing and wrestling were other school sports in which he dabbled.

After leaving school he became an apprentice pin-setter and when he joined Sedbergh Boys Club the little wrestling he had done as a schoolboy was brought out into the open. He moved on to the Windmill Wrestling Club, Manchester Road, a club that gave many well-known West Riding professionals their first leg-up in the sport. Now he was training seriously and success soon came his way. He won the Yorkshire Featherweight title aged seventeen, going on to retain the title the following year.

Jim decided to join the Army early rather than wait for his National Service call-up and signed on for three years with the Duke of Wellington's Regiment. Because of his fitness Jim was posted to the Physical Training Division, then back to the Regimental Depot at Halifax where he spent his service. On demob Jim went back to pin-setting at a textile mill, but the combined effects of the local depression in the industry and having a job he was not too keen on prompted him to rejoin the Army. However, a chance came via his famous ring friends, Bernard Murray and Norman Murrell, who encouraged him to become a professional wrestler in 1958.

So began the professional career of Jim Breaks that was to last some thirty years with around 5,000 professional bouts and many important titles. He took the European Lightweight Title (16 times), British Lightweight Title (8 times), British Welterweight Title (6 times) and the World Lightweight Title (twice), a truly remarkable record.

Jim Breaks was always a gentleman, a true professional ambassador for the wrestling business – a Yorkshireman who had time for the people who paid his wages and who achieved the correct balance between showmanship and humility.

Asa Briggs

Educationalist and Historian

Lord Briggs is one of Britain's foremost educationalists and historians. Such is the demand for his services from across the world that this lad from the back streets of Keighley became known as 'Lord Briggs of Heathrow'!

He was born in Emily Street, Keighley, in 1921. His father and grandfather were engineers and his mother's family farmed land at Oxenhope. A scholarship to Keighley Grammar School led young Asa to Cambridge University, a Double First in History and a First in Economics (the latter at the same time and in secret from his college!). After a brief spell of teaching at his old school he was called up into the Royal Corps of Signals and to Bletchley where he spent three years as part of the team that broke the Enigma code. After the war he accepted a fellowship at Oxford University where he later obtained a readership. While there he helped Winston Churchill write the monumental *History of the English-speaking Peoples*.

In 1955, and still only thirty-five, Asa Briggs became Professor of Modern History at Leeds University. Here he developed cross-departmental studies, a policy he continued to pursue when he was appointed Professor of History, Dean of Social Studies and Vice-Chancellor at the University of Sussex.

Sussex was one of the first 'new universities' planned for the 1960s, and under Professor Briggs's energetic and inspired leadership it led the way in modernising university study. In 1976, the year in which he was given a life peerage, he became Provost of Worcester College, Oxford. To this he added the post of Chancellor of the Open University (1978–94).

In this busy life Asa Briggs also produced a steady stream of highly regarded books, including *Victorian People*, *The Age of Improvement*, *Victorian Cities*, an official *History of Broadcasting in the UK* (in four volumes), and *A Social History of England*, which went to a second edition. He is on the editorial board of many journals and has officiated in numerous societies, including the Haworth-based Brontë Society (he was president for twenty years). Others are the Workers' Education Association, the Open University, the University Grants Committee, the Booker Committee, the Glyndebourne Trust, and the Victorian Society.

When speaking to the Library Association in 1971, Briggs commented that (even then) he had probably written more books than were in his childhood home in Emily Street. In this address Briggs paid tribute to the spirit of enquiry that had characterised the Keighley of his youth.

John Briggs MBE
Concert Pianist

John Briggs, Bingley's world-famous classical pianist, is a friend of princes and statesmen, but he has retained the wonderful outlook of his Yorkshire roots.

He was born in 1948 at Thornfield Nursing Home, Micklethwaite, near Bingley, and has never wanted to do anything but play the piano since the age of four. His first school was Crossflatts Junior and from there he went to Bingley Grammar School where he achieved three A-Levels. He went to the Royal Manchester College of Music for four years and earned a Teacher's Diploma. A short teaching career at Bingley College and Manchester High School for Girls followed.

In 1971 he won the Polish State Scholarship to study at the Warsaw Conservatoire but had only been there for three weeks when he was told he was to be deported. He was sent for by the Polish government and told to go, even though he had a contract for his period in Warsaw. John had not done anything to prompt deportation but had fallen victim to the latest rash of tit-for-tat expulsions that characterised this period of the Cold War – Harold Wilson's government had recently expelled 112 Soviet Embassy staff. After many James Bond-type escapades he finally managed to return home, albeit hounded by the national newspapers for some weeks. Controversy continued when the Polish cultural attaché was withdrawn from London – rumour had it 'Attaché, for John'!

John later studied with the famous Sulamita Aronovsky, a Professor from the Moscow Conservatory who had recently arrived in this country and was living in Shipley. He worked six or seven hours with her every day for fifteen months.

Over the years he has been one of Britain's most popular and professional pianists. He played a programme of Schumann, Chopin, Prokofiev, Liszt and Wagner at Carnegie Hall, New York, in 1987 and has also appeared at many other dramatic and unusual venues including Sydney Opera House, Cartagena Concert Hall, Colombia, and on the rim of the Grand Canyon. One of John's favourite performances was for the Jordanian royal family at Petra, where the rust-coloured temple and tombs are carved into the rocks on the edges of the Wadi Araba Desert.

An artist John holds in high esteem is the Swedish Wagnerian soprano Birgit Nilsson. When he was a young man he saw her perform *Electra* at the Covent Garden. Many years later, when he had his first television series, *John Briggs Music Show*, his first guest was Nilsson.

In the Queen's Birthday Honours List of 2003 John was awarded the MBE for his charitable work.

Anne Brontë

Novelist

Like her better-known sisters Charlotte and Emily, Anne Brontë was born in Thornton, Bradford. Soon after her birth on 17 January 1820 the family moved to Haworth where her father the Revd Patrick Brontë had been appointed minister. Anne's mother died the following year.

Unlike her sisters and brother, Anne remained in employment for many years, first at Blake Hall, Mirfield, then at Thorpe Green, Little Ouseburn (now Queen Ethelburga's School), as a governess. After joining with her sisters to publish a volume of poems in 1846, Anne's first novel appeared in 1847. Although it was overshadowed by Charlotte's *Jane Eyre* and Emily's *Wuthering Heights* (both published at the same time), *Agnes Grey* is less tempestuous and better crafted. It exposed the poor conditions under which governesses worked but was, nevertheless, an optimistic novel.

Anne's second novel, *The Tenant of Wildfell Hall*, was published in 1848. In it Anne highlighted the injustices suffered by a wife because of her lack of rights under the marriage laws of the time and portrayed her heroine's attempt to lead an independent life. As a result she was vilified as subversive and immoral. Subsequently, *The Tenant* has become one of the classics of feminist literature and Anne Brontë a leading figure in social history. She died of tuberculosis on 28 May 1849 aged twenty-nine, and was buried in St Mary's churchyard in Scarborough.

Charlotte Brontë

Novelist

Charlotte Brontë was born in Thornton, Bradford, on 21 April 1816 and lived most of her life in Haworth. Her experiences at the Clergy Daughters' School at Cowan Bridge, near Tunstall in Lancashire, in 1824–5 are immortalised as Lowood School in *Jane Eyre*. After two short spells as a governess, Charlotte (with Emily) went to Brussels in 1842–3 to gain experience to set up their own school in Haworth. No pupils were found, however, and the sisters turned to writing instead. After numerous rejections, Charlotte's novel *Jane Eyre* was published to great acclaim in 1847. After the deaths of her sisters Emily and Anne, and her brother Branwell, she wrote *Shirley* (published in 1849), describing life during Chartist times in the Dewsbury area (the 'Shirley' country). This was followed by *Villette*, an introspective autobiographical novel based on her time as a pupil in Brussels. Her fourth novel, *The Professor*, was published after her death.

Success as a novelist brought Charlotte increasing fame and wealth, though most of her time was spent looking after her elderly and infirm father, the Revd Patrick Brontë, Vicar of Haworth. In 1854 Charlotte married her father's curate, the Revd

Arthur Nicholls, but died on 31 March the following year from complications during pregnancy. She is buried in Haworth Parish Church.

In 1857 Elizabeth Gaskell's *Life of Charlotte Brontë* was published, immortalising the Brontë story.

Emily Brontë

Novelist

Emily Jane Brontë was born in Thornton, Bradford, on 30 July 1818, but apart from brief stays at school Cowan Bridge, Roe Head, Southowram and Brussels, lived all her life in the parsonage at Haworth.

In reviews of the volume of poems published with her sisters in 1846, Emily's received the greatest acclaim. 'No Coward Soul Is Mine' is perhaps her most famous. In 1847 *Wuthering Heights*, her one and only novel, was published. This complex saga of family feuding and cruelty was heavily criticised on publication as coarse and vulgar. It has since become the most translated novel of all time and has been filmed many times; it has even been performed as an opera and a ballet. Heathcliff and Cathy are cultural icons. Emily, like her novel, remains elusive and enigmatic.

On 19 December 1848 Emily died at the parsonage of consumption aged twenty-nine and was buried in Haworth parish church.

Haworth Parsonage.

Barbara Castle

Politician

Baroness Castle, the left-wing, flame-headed political tornado, was the best-known woman parliamentarian of her day, and once looked like becoming Britain's first female prime minister. She remained a tireless active politician well into her eighties.

She was born Barbara Anne Betts in Chesterfield, Derbyshire, on 6 October 1910. Her family moved to Hull and later Pontefract before settling in Bradford. Her father was Frank Betts, a civil servant in the tax department, a socialist and editor of the *Bradford Pioneer*. The family lived in Toller Lane, Heaton.

Educated at Bradford Girls' Grammar School, she won a scholarship to Oxford University. She later became involved in local government as a borough councillor with St Pancras Borough Council in 1937. In 1944 she married Ted Castle, a fellow labour activist and former *Daily Mirror* journalist. She was widowed in 1979.

During the war she was employed at the Ministry of Food and in 1945 she entered parliament as a Labour MP for Blackburn. There she became known for her outspoken support of socialist causes and served as chairman of the Labour Party from 1958 to 1959.

After the Labour Party's election victory in 1964, she joined the cabinet of Harold Wilson, first as Minister of Overseas Development (1964–5), then as Minister of Transport (1965–8). In the latter post she was responsible for the introduction of the breath test for drink drivers. As the first Secretary of State for Employment and Production (1968–70) she courted controversy with her proposals for trade union reform set out in a white paper. With hindsight, the rejection of these proposals is often held to have sealed the fate of Labour and the unions in the late 1970s and '80s.

She remained in the Shadow Cabinet during the Conservative government of the early 1970s and when Labour regained power in 1974 she became Secretary of State for Social Services. However, when James Callaghan replaced Wilson as prime minister in 1976 she was banished to the back benches and left Westminster to become a Member of the European Parliament.

She was given an honorary doctorate in technology by Bradford University in 1968, and was made an honorary fellow of Bradford and Ilkley Community College in 1985. In 1990 she became a life peer and in 1997 received the highest honour it was possible to bestow in Bradford, the Freedom of the City.

Baroness Castle of Blackburn died in May 2002 aged ninety-one.

Garth Cawood

Showbusiness Entrepreneur and Theatrical Agent

Garth Cawood was probably one of the earliest ballroom disc jockeys in the UK. He began his career at the Tudor Ballroom, Dudley Hill, in the mid-1950s, where he used an old-style (although modern then) radiogram, which held eight 78rpm records. While the machine was making the automatic change between discs Garth would give some type of introduction. It was primitive, but it worked – and he became the forerunner of the modern disco DJ.

Born on 27 August 1940 at 155 Apperley Road, Idle, Garth attended Greengates Primary School, and St Barnabas School, Heaton, when the family moved to Victor Road. Later, when his parents took over the Tudor Ballroom, he attended Buttershaw School and after numerous other moves the family finally made their home at 2 Sturgess Grove, Undercliffe.

Garth left school at fifteen and joined the *Telegraph & Argus* as a trainee press photographer. After four years he moved to well-known Bradford photographers Eric's, situated in the Mechanics' Institute opposite the Town Hall. In the late 1950s he joined The Dingos, a local skiffle group. Garth had seen them many times at his parents' ballroom, and while they were clearly quite talented, he quickly recognised that their organisation and professionalism were not so hot. At the end of each number played, for example, there was no thank you or introduction to the next song. Garth's arrival turned The Dingos Skiffle Group into one of the most professional and entertaining groups in Yorkshire.

After a few years it was time to move on, and with his talent as a compère he was soon in demand from the many package shows performing at cinemas and other venues around the UK. He soon became a top name compère and friend of the Beatles, the Rolling Stones, the Searchers and many other top artists of the time. He also had disc jockey spots at the Gaumont and the Majestic in Bradford, and was the first DJ at the new Mecca on Manningham Lane.

After all this experience in the mid-1960s he spent five years at Brigitte Bardot's club Esquade in St Tropez, organising and entertaining the wealthy. Because of his contacts in show business, in his spare time he was organising contracts, booking bands and stars from the UK to Europe and vice versa.

In 1970 Garth was back in the UK in his capacity as compère, notably at the Savoy Club, Wakefield, Batley Variety Club and Keighley Variety Club, all top cabaret venues. During this period he lived at his parents' home at Sturgess Grove which became a travel stop for many artists of the time. These included Tom Jones, Gene Vincent, Jess Conrad, Carl Denver and many others.

He was now working with his own house band, The Mike Stuart Sound, and for a few months had a permanent position working six days a week at the Lyceum (Talk of Yorkshire). From there they moved to a four-day week at the Keighley Variety Club. During this time Garth and the band brought a 'theatrical illusion' act to the concerts, 'a showground experience with music'. Building on their success he

and his business partner Stuart Reynolds purchased the Keighley Variety Club, changing its name to The Funhouse Bar. They then acquired the Flying Dutchman Club in Leeds Road, Bradford, and changed its name to Funny's, a fun pub with continental overtones. The constant stream of guest stars included Garth's good friend Diana Dors and many of the cast of *Coronation Street*.

In 1984 they sold both businesses and Garth went on tour with the house band under the new title Garth Cawood's Fun House. It was in the late 1980s that Garth and Stuart formed the Fun House Theatrical Agency. They now represent a formidable list of TV and theatre personalities. Many of the contestants on *Stars in Their Eyes* have found the agency has promoted their careers, including Garry Mullen, all-time record winner with his tribute to Freddie Mercury of Queen.

One of Garth's most treasured memories is the time he spent with the Beatles, an experience recorded in a photograph of him with the group during his days as a compère.

Private George W. Chafer VC

Victoria Cross Recipient, First World War

George Chafer was born at 77 Mill Lane, West Bowling, Bradford, on 16 April 1894. His mother Alice was a domestic servant. At an early age he moved with his mother to Epworth, Lincolnshire, but was orphaned shortly afterwards and brought up by his aunt, Mrs Brooks of Rotherham. He subsequently made his home with Mr and Mrs Reed of 15 Silverwood Cottages and was employed as a weigh clerk at the Silverwood Colliery in Rotherham.

George William Chafer joined the East Yorkshire Regiment on 2 June 1915 and was given the regimental number 19384. When he joined the army he was so small in physique that his friends ridiculed the idea of his being accepted. After six months training at home with the 3rd Battalion he was sent to the front, drafted to the 1st Battalion and posted to 'C' Company.

In the months that followed Chafer proved himself a good soldier, never in trouble and very useful in his platoon. Noted early by the platoon officer for his coolness and smartness, he was made a bomber. So far there was nothing remarkable about Chafer, but a critical moment was coming that enabled him to show his bravery.

At Meaulte in France, on 3–4 June 1916, 'C' Company was subjected to horrific experiences. The scene was terrible: one trench had been almost levelled by shellfire and enemy mortars. It was being swept by machine-gun fire and the air was poisoned by gas fumes. Chafer was lying seriously wounded in hand and leg, bruised and dazed by concussion, choking and blinded by gas, when he saw a soldier coming along with a written message. Another shellburst partially buried this orderly, who shouted, 'Someone take this message for the captain.' There was no man left alive within hearing range except Chafer.

He took the message from the soldier, and as the trench had been knocked in so badly, crawled on to the parapet in spite of excruciating pain. There were shells, bullets from machine-guns and rifles raining around him, and it is a miracle that he came through without further injury. The first living occupant of the trench Chafer reached was a corporal. The latter could hardly believe his eyes when he saw a man wearing a gas helmet, his left hand shot through and bleeding profusely, still clutching his rifle and dragging himself painfully along the parapet with one leg torn by shell wounds, crying out all the time, 'A message for the captain'. After handing it over, Chafer collapsed. He was awarded the Victoria Cross, the highest honour his country could bestow. The citation in the *London Gazette* of 5 August 1916 states: 'He displayed great initiative and splendid devotion to duty at a critical moment.'

In a moment of crisis, forced to choose between ordinary and extraordinary action, Chafer chose the highest and best course open to him and achieved the seemingly impossible. His magnificent devotion to duty at all costs, at the imminent

risk of paying the supreme sacrifice of his life, could only have been adequately rewarded by the Victoria Cross.

George William Chafer VC died in Rotherham General Hospital on Tuesday 1 March 1966 at the age of seventy. The funeral service took place at Bramley Parish Church on Friday 4 March 1966, followed by cremation. He was the East Yorkshire Regiment's last surviving holder of the Victoria Cross.

Brian Close CBE

Yorkshire, Somerset and England Cricketer

Brian Close is one of the few sports celebrities who could be described as 'a legend in his own lifetime'. His deeds in cricket are legend, controversy has surrounded him, but he was a master strategist as captain of Yorkshire, inspiring them to win four County Championships in 1963, 1966, 1967 and 1968, plus Gillette Cup wins in 1965 and 1969.

Brian was born in Town Street, Rawdon, on 24 February 1931. His father Harry worked as a weaver in nearby Guiseley, playing cricket for Undercliffe in the Bradford League. Brian's first school was Rawdon Littlemoor Junior and he then moved to Aireborough Grammar. During this time he played cricket for Guiseley and Yeadon in the Airedale & Wharfedale League.

At school he was an outstanding pupil, passing his Higher School Certificate. So proficient was he at maths that his headmaster wanted him to study the subject at Cambridge. However, this would not have been possible until he had completed his National Service. This delay was to have important implications for his career: cricket was to be his life.

His versatility as a sportsman was evident in his fledgling years. Success as a footballer matched his cricket achievements and in the early days he was better known as a promising soccer talent than as a cricketer with a future. It was a time when it was possible to juggle the two sports, and many did so. At the age of fourteen Brian was on Leeds United's books as an amateur. Twelve months later he toured Holland with a West Riding FA Youth XI and subsequently became the first Leeds product to play for an England Youth Team. In October 1948 he represented England against Scotland at Pittodrie Park in Aberdeen.

When the time came for his National Service he was posted to the Royal Signals at Catterick. A football injury had caused the postponement of his call-up and this meant he could take the opportunity to play for Yorkshire County Cricket Club at the start of the 1949 season. Maurice Webb, the Bradford MP and cricket enthusiast, acting on behalf of Yorkshire, was able to use his influence to obtain deferment of Close's National Service until the end of the season, thus ensuring Brian's memorable entry into first-class cricket.

Close still holds the record for the youngest player to represent England when, after a superb all-round first season with Yorkshire, he was selected to play against New Zealand at eighteen. He never fully realised the promise of that first season, being in and out of the England side for the next twenty-seven years. Batting left- and bowling right-handed, he completed the double (1,000 runs and 100 wickets) in 1949, the youngest player to do so. As a batsman he could defend with great obduracy, but could attack thrillingly, although not always wisely. He bowled medium pace and offspin with more consistency than he batted.

He lost favour with the England selectors after trying to hit Richie Benaud out of the attack in the 1961 Old Trafford Test, but returned to take England to the brink

of victory in the 1963 Lord's Test against the West Indies. He captained Yorkshire and England with success, but again lost the England position after being accused of delaying tactics in a county game. Later, internal politics saw him move from Yorkshire to Somerset for the final years of his career.

His cricketing record is almost without equal. In all he played 536 matches for Yorkshire between 1949 and 1970 (captain 1963–70); 142 matches for Somerset (captain 1971–7); 22 matches for England 1949–76 (captain seven times). His highest batting score was 198 (Yorkshire v. Surrey at The Oval in 1960), best bowling figures 8–41 (Yorkshire v. Kent at Headingley in 1959). His career record amounts to 34,994 runs (average 33.26) with 52 centuries; 1,171 wickets (average 26.42 runs); and 813 catches. In 1964 he was Wisden Cricketer of the Year and in 1975 he was awarded the CBE for his services to cricket. Towards the end of his career he was an England selector and chairman of the Yorkshire committee.

Now fully retired, he lives in Baildon and has a phenomenal recall of his eventful life. It has been said that the Yorkshire side has never been the same since his move, and certainly the team he captained then has had no serious rival in the county's history.

Ian Clough

Mountaineer

On 30 May 1970 a giant tower of ice collapsed on thirty-year-old climber Ian Clough just as the last party of climbers were leaving Annapurna in the Himalayas.

Born in Baildon in 1940, Ian Clough lived with his parents in Cornwall Crescent and as a boy he used to climb the steep sides of The Bank near his home. This was the beginning of a career that added glittering exploits to British mountaineering history. He was educated at Sandal Secondary School, Baildon, and Bingley Grammar School. Joining the Westgate Methodist Scout Group where his proficiency earned him Queen's Scout status, it was with the Baildon Scout Group that he went to the climbing hut at Kandersdeg in Switzerland, founded by Lord Baden-Powell. After this he had no fear of heights and from then on his parents never saw him at weekends.

From seventeen onwards he was rock climbing and making a name for himself. Ian did his National Service in the Royal Air Force and extended this to three years when he became a member of the RAF Mountain Rescue Service. It was at this time that he gained much valuable experience on ice and snow in Scotland.

With many peaks conquered, in 1962 he attempted one of the most difficult climbs with his famous climbing companion Chris Bonington – the north face of the Eiger. Despite twice taking the wrong route, which they had to abandon, they fought their way to the top. It could have been a record climb but for the three-hour delay that resulted from getting lost. They stood proudly on the magnificent Eiger after twenty hours of ascent, and came back down in only one and a half hours, a truly tremendous feat.

Ian was later a member of Chris Bonington's British team in a successful ascent of The Fortress, an 11,000ft peak in the icy storm-swept wastes of Patagonia near the tip of South America. It was a shining example of boldness and high adventure. Ian said later, 'This previously unclimbed mountain was much more difficult than the north wall of the Eiger, with gales of 120mph, and powdered snow which made the rock as slippery as glass.'

On 30 May 1970 Ian was with a group of climbers led by Chris Bonington. They had successfully conquered the south face of Annapurna in the Himalayas, an ascent considered by experts to be a tougher climb than Everest itself. It was on the descent that the tragedy occurred. Ian and his companion Michael Thompson had been carrying light gear. Their route lay beneath a long ice cliff with an overhang that had fallen away about a month before and no longer seemed to be a danger. However, the ice did start to move again. Ian was four paces in front of Thompson who was able to rush back and out of danger. It was too late for Ian: he was caught in the main pack of the avalanche, only four steps away from survival.

He was later buried in a grassy hollow near base camp, where the expedition's porters made a wreath of blue alpine flowers which were placed on the grave; the sherpas built a wooden cross with a cairn around it.

In 1971 a public hall and new library in Baildon were named after Ian and opened by his colleague Chris Bonington. In November 1999 a special commemorative plaque to Yorkshire's most famous climber was erected at Annapurna base camp.

John Coates

Tenor

Singers are notorious casualties along Memory Lane. Like other practitioners of temporary and ephemeral arts, they take their secrets with them into retirement and oblivion. One such person was John Coates, friend of Elgar and one of England's greatest tenors.

He was born on 29 June 1865 in Girlington Road, and his family later moved to 42 Carlisle Place. His father was a choirmaster at Girlington Parish Church, his mother, a well-known soprano at Manningham Parish Church, sang in various musical societies and taught John to sing. Before he was five John could sight-read music and in 1870 he became a chorister at Manningham.

At the age of eight he started at Bradford Grammar School. A singing class was formed and John would sing solos at the school concerts. He soon became leader and soloist in the church choir and remained there until the age of seventeen when his voice broke. When his father died in 1877 at the age of thirty-seven, John, then twelve, had to leave Bradford Grammar School to work as an office boy in a Bradford warehouse earning six shillings a week. Later he was employed in a yarn merchant's office. His spare time was largely devoted to the study of modern languages.

In 1893, aged twenty-eight, with savings of £50, he took his wife and family to London to establish a career as a singer. He tried to get into the Carl Rosa Opera Company as a baritone, but the directors did not consider his voice strong enough for grand opera. He took lessons with Mr William Shakespeare who suggested he would be better as a tenor rather than a baritone. After a struggle for recognition he started singing in comic operas for the D'Oyly Carte Opera Company, earning £8 a week. In 1894 they sent him to America where he appeared as Mr Goldbury in *Utopia Limited* in New York and Boston.

Returning to England, still with the D'Oyly Carte, he appeared in many successful roles until 1895, when he left the company. There followed a series of engagements in musical comedy in London and the provinces, and a second visit to America. Now convinced he was really a tenor and not a baritone, in 1899 Coates gave up the stage temporarily, and began studying a variety of tenor parts in private. It was during this period that he sang Sullivan's song 'The Absent-minded Beggar' at the Alhambra Theatre, Bradford, in 1899.

He soon became one of the most successful singers in England, performing in many cities. He also made a name for himself as an operatic tenor, travelling with the Moody Manners' Company in 1907–8, and with the Beecham opera companies of 1910 and 1911. He went on tours of the UK, South Africa and Australia from 1911 to 1913.

Despite being above military age he joined the Officer Training Corps in November 1914 and was given a commission with the Yorkshire Regiment in the First World War, spending a year at the front in France. Discharged with the rank

of captain he resumed his professional career in 1919. After the war he was active principally as a concert singer, specialising in Elizabethan and Tudor composers.

He appeared infrequently on stage after 1930 but broadcast on radio over fifty times and entranced listeners with his lectures. He had a beautiful garden and bird sanctuary at his home in Northwood, Middlesex, and it was there, after a long illness, that he died aged seventy-six in August 1941.

Harry Corbett OBE

The Creator of Sooty

A little yellow bear named Sooty was one of the UK's first children's television superstars and for well over fifty years his antics have brought entertainment to whole generations of appreciative younger viewers.

Harry Corbett, the creator of Britain's most celebrated glove puppet, was born on 28 January 1918 at 21 Edmund Street, just a few hundred yards from the Alhambra Theatre in Bradford, which may have had something to do with his becoming an entertainer. His father was a miner for many years but later took a fish and chip shop in Bradford. His uncle, Harry Ramsden, also had two fish shops in Bradford, and then moved to a small wooden hut at the back of the White Cross Hotel, Guiseley.

Harry Corbett attended Carlton High School, Bradford. When he left at the age of sixteen he started work as an apprentice in the electric motor works at Crompton Parkinson, Guiseley. He and his family lived for a short time in Oxford Road, Guiseley, but later made their home above a fish and chip shop in Springfield Road.

After working for Crompton Parkinson's for thirteen years, he joined the Vulcan Boiler Insurance Company as an engineer/surveyor, and it was during this time that he took up amateur conjuring and magic, doing shows throughout the district.

Sooty's life began in July 1948 when just Harry bought the original glove puppet for *7s 6d* from a toy shop on the North Pier at Blackpool to amuse his own children. Harry was no ventriloquist, and as the show was originally just Harry and Sooty there was no way for him to make the bear speak, so Sooty didn't utter a word to the audience, he whispered to Harry.

Harry soon set about incorporating the puppet into his magic act with immediate success and it was in 1952 that the mismatched duo made their first TV debut on a BBC show called *Talent Night*. A star was born.

In 1968 the BBC decided to drop *The Sooty Show* and Harry and Sooty signed for Thames TV, but on Christmas Day 1975 Harry suffered a massive heart attack and his son Matthew had to take over as Sooty's mentor.

Harry Corbett was awarded the OBE in the New Years Honours List in 1976, and accepted it from Queen Elizabeth while recuperating from his heart attack. Sooty also went to Buckingham Palace to accept a miniature OBE medal. In August 1989 Harry Corbett passed away at his home in Child Okeford, near Blandford, Dorset, aged seventy-one.

Bob Cryer

Member of Parliament

Non-smoking, teetotal, agnostic and committed socialist, a man who wanted to make a difference to the lives of those less fortunate, who never lost touch with his constituents, respected by all parties, this was Keighley's MP Bob Cryer.

George Robert Cryer was born on 3 December 1934 at 18 Kelsall Terrace, Great Horton. The family soon moved to 15 Albert Road, Saltaire, Shipley, where Bob attended Albert Road Junior School, moving on to Salt's Grammar School. He completed his education at Hull University, where he read economics. He played cricket for Great Horton and was a member of the team that won the Priestley Shield in 1955.

He trained as a teacher and taught at secondary schools in Hull and briefly at Keighley. He also lectured at technical colleges in Blackburn, Dewsbury and Keighley from 1965 until the early 1970s.

He moved to Keighley in the 1960s and became a member of the old Keighley Borough Council from 1971 to 1974. It was in 1974 that Bob captured Keighley from the Conservative Joan Hall to become a Member of Parliament. In 1976 he was promoted to be a junior minister in the Department of Industry, but in November resigned from his ministerial post complaining that the government's manifesto promises were not being fulfilled, in particular objecting to the refusal to fund the Kirkby Workers' Co-operative.

In the general election of 1979 he nearly lost his seat with a majority of only seventy-eight after two recounts. In 1983, an election year in which the Conservatives' Commons majority went up to 144, he inevitably lost Keighley. In 1984 he was elected as the MEP for Sheffield and held the post until 1989, during which time he constantly urged Britain's withdrawal from Europe. In 1987 he returned to Westminster as the member for Bradford South, after another narrow victory (a majority of 309 votes) and retained the seat easily in 1992.

Perhaps one of Bob Cryer's permanent legacies is the work he did on the Keighley & Worth Valley Railway Preservation Society, of which he was a founder member in 1962, and its first chairman. So enthusiastic was he that during his spare time after six years' experience as a fireman, he then qualified as an engine driver and was a supporter of the railway right up until his untimely death in a road accident on 12 April 1994 aged fifty-nine. There is a plaque to Bob's memory on Haworth station.

Kiki Dee

International Singing Star

Kiki's impeccable vocal abilities have established her impressive credentials as a musician during a career that covers four decades.

Kiki was born Pauline Matthews on 6 March 1947 at the family home, 146 Marsh Street, Little Horton. Pauline first attended St Oswald's Primary School, then Wibsey Secondary School, where she admits to being pretty average. From an early age Pauline was encouraged by her father to sing (she was a natural), and by the age of ten she was winning local talent contests and establishing herself as a star in Yorkshire. At sixteen, Pauline left school to pursue her dream, and began singing in a dance band in Leeds. It was during this time that she adopted her stage name, Kiki Dee, by taking the style of knee-high 'kinky boots' that were fashionable at that time and adding the American actress Sandra Dee's last name.

In 1964 she was scouted by Philips Fontana who released her debut recording of Mitch Murray's 'Early Night' the same year. After a slow start she made her debut album I'm Kiki Dee in 1968, and in 1970 she became the first British female singer to sign for the Motown label.

In 1973 Elton John signed her to his Rocket label, and her single 'Amoureuse' reached number thirteen in the charts. A year later, in 1974, she formed the Kiki Dee Band. Her first album recording, *I've Got the Music in Me*, went gold in the USA. In 1976 Kiki returned to follow up the hit album and recorded a duet with Elton John, the world smash hit 'Don't Go Breaking My Heart'.

In 1978 Kiki recorded her final disc for the newly RCA-renovated Rocket Records, 'Stay with Me'. In 1984 she made her West End debut in the international production *Pump Boys and Dinettes*. She received rave reviews and then an Olivier Awards nomination for her performance as Mrs Johnstone in the revival of the hit musical *Blood Brothers*.

After several years in and out of the spotlight, Kiki returned to the charts in 1993 via a Top Ten duet with Elton John, when they sang the Cole Porter classic 'True Love'. She followed this up with an anthology album of songs from throughout her career.

With her musical partner, guitarist and songwriter Carmelo Luggeri, she has been creating original music for the last few years. Their recordings varying from the live 'Almost Naked', featuring only voice and guitar, to the haunting production of 'Where Rivers Meet' with its texture of east–west influences.

This daughter of a weaving overlooker, who as Pauline Matthews turned her back on a job as a counter assistant at Boots in Broadway, Bradford, became the queen of British rock and a world star.

Frederick Delius CH
Composer

Despite spending most of his sixty-seven years living abroad, Frederick Delius became ranked as a quint-essentially English composer along with Ralph Vaughan-Williams, William Walton and Sir Edward Elgar.

Affectionately known at home as Fritz, he was born on 29 January 1862 at 1–3 Claremont, Great Horton, of German parents from Westphalia, who came to Bradford to make their fortune in the textile industry. Julius was a wool manufacturer and one of a group of Germans who arranged for Manchester's Hallé Orchestra to visit St George's Hall. Often musicians were invited to the Deliuses' home. Frederick, aged seven, started violin lessons and played for the great Joseph Joachim, but his father had no intention of allowing his son to become a professional musician.

Frederick was sent to Bradford Grammar School, where he disliked most subjects except geography and languages. After leaving the grammar school he worked in his father's wool business for over three years as a travelling representative, but his interest in music continued to consume his thoughts. His frustrated father thought a change of business might inspire greater industry in his son and sent Fritz to an orange plantation in Florida. There he took more interest in black music and women than the cultivation of oranges. He quickly secured a piano and found a local source for theory lessons. Delius stayed in Florida for 18 months before moving to Danville, Virginia, with sufficient confidence to teach music in his own right.

Julius now gave in to his son's request for a full musical education, and so Fritz enrolled at the Leipzig Conservatorium where he studied from 1886 to 1888 before moving to Paris in 1890.

For much of his life Delius worked in obscurity, though Thomas Beecham, Henry Wood, and other eminent conductors championed his music. Slowly but surely his fame grew, and for the next forty years he lived with his wife Jelka in the village of Grez-sur-Loing, south of Paris. Little could be done to help the composer's failing health, though, for Delius began to go blind and gradually lost the use of his limbs. Ultimately, he could no longer compose.

In 1928 a young musician from Yorkshire, Eric Fenby, came to live in Grez with the Deliuses, and during his last years the composer completed a number of works by dictation.

Delius was made Companion of Honour in 1929 and his home town made him a Freeman of the City. Leeds University gave him an honorary D.Litt.

Frederick Delius died at Grez-sur-Loing on 10 June 1934, his wife outliving him by just one year. They are buried at Limpsfield, Surrey.

Sandra Dorne

Actress

Husky-voiced Sandra Dorne secured lead roles in the 1950s and was a popular pin-up early in her career. Appearing in some thirty-five films and many television plays, she specialised in mystery, suspense and horror.

She was born Joanna Smith on 19 June 1925 at 19 Aylesbury Street, Ingrow, Keighley, a back-to-back house in the shadow of St John the Evangelist, Ingrow's parish church. She attended Ingrow Primary School.

As a youngster she sang in concerts, often performing songs written by her father Harry Smith, a local entertainer. Soon she was playing chorus and pantomime roles in the theatres and music halls in the district. She changed her name to Sandrea Dawn, later to Sandra Dorne when she played the title role in *Cinderella* at the Regal Theatre, Southport, and became known as the 'the girl with long golden tresses'.

The Second World War and its aftermath was a lively time for low-budget British films, the 'B features', and by 1945 Sandra had appeared in *Women in Sport* and *We, the People*. In 1946 the newly formed Brighton Film Company were on the lookout for new talent and gave her a three-year contract. Over the next four years Sandra made five films, and was given a major role in the 1951 film *Happy Go Lovely*, which starred Cesar Romero and David Niven.

Now a star and a pin-up, her glamour picture appeared in *Picturegoer* magazine and on Pathé newsreels. Who would be better to play Sukey Tawdrey in Peter Brook's 1952 film version of *The Beggar's Opera* than the new British 'blonde bombshell' Sandra Dorne? She was now sharing the screen with many famous names: Dirk Bogarde, Laurence Olivier, Dorothy Tutin, John Gielgud and even Bob Hope (in *The Iron Petticoat*).

In 1954, she married the British actor Patrick Holt (1912–96). Her film career spanned over forty years, continuing well into the late 1980s. Her 100-plus TV appearances included roles in *The Avengers*, *Mark Saber*, *Dial 999*, many plays and ABC TV's *Armchair Theatre*. She was never as famous as such sex symbol contemporaries as Diana Dors (her lifelong friend) and Marilyn Monroe, and was always cast as a trollop, a good-time girl, or as the 'other woman'.

In 1951 the famous sculptor Jacob Epstein modelled her head and shoulders in a work he called *Dawn*. He thought her face 'both childlike and beautiful'. The bust was exhibited in London in 1952, but today its whereabouts is unknown.

Sandra Dorne died on Christmas Day 1992, aged sixty-seven.

Bob Duckett

Author and Librarian

Bob Duckett is a man of letters, who adopted Bradford and has spent over thirty years researching the city's heritage.

Born in 1942 in Llanelli, South Wales, he was educated at Purley County Grammar School, Surrey, the University of Strathclyde, Glasgow (where he secured library qualifications), the University of Leicester where he gained a BA (Hons) in philosophy, and Leeds Polytechnic (MA in librarianship).

Captivated by its Victorian architecture, glimpses of moorland, and the cherry blossom trees then surrounding the City Hall, Bob decided to stay in Bradford and work for the library service.

It was from his appointment as Reference Librarian in 1985 that Bob started to make his presence felt on Bradford's publishing scene. He has been responsible for over forty books, ranging from *The Siege of Bradford* (the one in 1643!) and *The Domes of Delight* (about the Alhambra) to the 2002 publications *Riddlesden* and the geography textbook *The Bradford Region*. Beyond the library service, Bob has edited the *Bradford Antiquary* and two volumes of *Aspects of Bradford*. He rescued the journal *Library History* from bankruptcy (he was Treasurer of the Library History Society at the time) and did the same for *Brontë Studies: Journal of the Brontë Society*. Now it has some 2,000 subscribers worldwide.

Bob's involvement with the Brontë Society came about as a result of helping an enquirer in the library. It was clear that in his role as a librarian he could be of help to the society and he was elected to its governing council; he now has the longest continuous service of any of the council's members. Bob was also a founding member of the J.B. Priestley Society. He is Honorary Publications Officer for both these societies, and has helped with editing and marketing. Rarely, though, will you find Bob's name in these books; he sees himself as a 'facilitator'.

In the professional library field Bob is well known, and not just for his writing. He won a prize for the best article of 1994 (on reference libraries), wrote a best-seller (with two staff colleagues) called *Know It All: Find It Fast* in 2002 for the Library Association, and has written 40 articles and 500 book reviews. He is a frequent referee and prize panellist, so he is kept pretty busy! He has spoken at many conferences, served on national committees and working parties, and been a friendly mentor to many a grateful member of staff and member of the public.

So what kept Bob here? 'The moors, challenge of the job and a growing family. Bradford's been a great place and been good to me. Everywhere I go I see people I know, and I owe Bradford Libraries a lot.' Bradford owes Bob, too.

Andrea Dunbar
Playwright

Based in the ground floor of the Central Library is The Write Place, which provides equipment and space for local writers to work. The room is quiet and self-contained – a tribute to the short life and work of Andrea Dunbar.

She was born in Bradford in 1961 and lived at Brafferton Arbor on the Buttershaw estate with her parents and seven brothers and sisters. When she was fifteen and a pupil at Buttershaw Comprehensive School she wrote *Arbor*, her first play, for her CSE examination, with much encouragement from her teachers. It was raw stuff: adolescents drifting aimlessly through school against a background of poverty, overcrowding, violence and the dim social workers they attracted.

Three years later the play was staged at the Royal Court's Theatre Upstairs in London, and with its success she was encouraged to write more for the stage. After leaving school, she worked as a sewing machinist, and on French combing at Bowling Mills, Manchester Road, but moved into the theatre full time under a Youth Opportunities Scheme with the Impact Theatre Group of Leeds.

Leaving the family home, she moved to a council flat on the Braithwaite estate in Keighley. After *Arbor* came the follow-up, *Rita, Sue and Bob Too*, which was also performed at the Royal Court. It gained an award for young writers. Her work so impressed the producer Sandy Lieberson that he decided to make a film through his company Umbrella Entertainment Productions. It was financed by Channel 4.

After a one-off showing at the Brighton Festival in 1987 it was viewed with resentment in Bradford after sensational Fleet Street stories about its content. But when the film was actually shown in the city, the crowds rushed to see it. The setting is depressing: Bradford's Buttershaw is grim and desolate, a place where people's lives seem to be without any sort of hope, but in spite of this *Rita, Sue and Bob Too* is often extremely funny and won over residents with its warmth and earthy humour. It had already won praise at the Cannes Film Festival, and Andrea was destined to become an international celebrity.

Sadly, in 1990, when she had just started a sequel roughly based on the same characters and again set in Buttershaw, she collapsed in her local pub The Beacon and later died in hospital of a brain haemorrhage aged only twenty-nine. Despite her fame she never made a fortune out of her writing and was still living on Buttershaw estate on social security when she died.

She had already achieved success, something that eludes many playwrights in a long working lifetime, and she steeped herself in a distinctive area and made it her own.

Richard Dunn

Boxer and World Heavyweight Title Contender

Bradfordians have always had a special place in their affections for the brave heavyweight boxer Richard Dunn. Few will forget the memorable night of 25 May 1976 in Munich when Dunn, then aged thirty-one, met the greatest boxer of his generation, Muhammad Ali.

Richard was born on 19 January 1945 in St James' Hospital, Leeds; the family was then living in Meanwood. He was the youngest of eleven children and never knew his father, who was killed during the war. As a youngster, his early years were spent in Bramley. At school his favourite subjects were PT, religious instruction and history.

He left school at fifteen for the building site – the working man's body-building school. On the site he weighed in at 112lb, but suddenly shot up in height and soon his weight and strength started to increase. In successive jobs he handled road drills for Halifax Corporation and became a linesman's mate for the Yorkshire Electricity Board. For recreation he joined the Territorial Army as a member of 4th Battalion Parachute Regiment at Thornbury Barracks, and played amateur rugby league for St Mary's Church team as a loose forward. He turned down offers from Halifax, Huddersfield, Bradford Northern and Oldham rugby league clubs.

His future outlook changed after a visit to Halifax Star Boxing Club, where he met his future father-in-law, boxing trainer Jim Devanney. Although boxing was not yet on his priority list, he was sufficiently tempted to put in occasional appearances for the Star under Jim's wing. Dunn's first amateur fight was at a Bradford club where he had a first-round knock-out and won a casserole dish! He travelled to Doncaster the following month and won a wall-clock after a similar pattern of events. The same month he was matched against a docker in Hull and tasted his first defeat, losing on points. Still with the Paras and rugby league, his programme was becoming too crowded and he therefore decided his rugby playing days and drops from the sky must be sacrificed in favour of boxing.

In 1969, after many months in amateur boxing and disappointment at being overlooked on the national scene, he decided to turn professional. It was at this time that Richard, his wife and son moved into a corporation house at Buttershaw, and two years later, into his own home in Undercliffe. He was thirty before he claimed the British and Commonwealth titles with a gruelling 15-round points win over Bunny Johnson at Wembley. He defended his titles by stopping Danny McAlinden in two rounds, and followed this up by gaining a three-round win over German Bernd August to claim the European crown. That clinched the former building worker a £100,000 pay day against Ali who had just regained his crown with an epic win over George Foreman in Zaire.

Dunn was a 7–1 outsider. The fight itself was brief but action-packed. Dunn, cheered on by an army of Bradfordians who had made the trip to Munich, stunned Ali with a big right and two left-hand punches in the third round. Ali responded by

flooring Dunn three times in the fourth. Each time Dunn hauled himself up and battled on. In the fifth he again showed great courage as he somehow hauled himself off the canvas twice, despite counts of nine and eight, before hitting the deck for a final time at which point the referee stopped the fight.

Dunn returned home to a hero's reception. Bradford Council honoured him by naming the sports centre constructed at Odsal after him. After retiring from his 45-fight career which saw him record 33 wins, Richard and his family left Westfield Lane, Wrose, and invested £90,000 of his earnings in the 43-roomed Attenborough Hotel in Scarborough, but four years later he was forced to sell up. He then went to work on the oil-rigs, but a bad fall left him with two shattered legs. Yet Dunn is a man who never lost his sense of humour or the affection of the Bradford people.

Ali paid the ultimate tribute to his bravery, saying, 'Dunn was a proud man. I figured he would run, but he didn't know the meaning of fear.'

Francis Durbridge

Author

Were the seeds of an idea that led to the creation of Paul Temple sown in Bradford's Kirkgate Market and Swan Arcade in the 1920s?

Francis Durbridge was born 1912 in Hull. He decided at the age of twelve to be a writer, buying every second-hand book he could from the stalls in both the Swan Arcade and Kirkgate Market. In those days his father worked for Woolworth's in Bradford and in the two years that Francis lived in the city he was a pupil at Bradford Grammar School. In later life he said that he had many happy memories of his time in Bradford, and that the bookstalls were very important to him.

It was in 1938 that Durbridge created Paul Temple, the suave, gentlemanly scourge of murderers, whose weekly cliff-hanging radio shows had Britain holding its breath. Many people will remember their introduction to Paul Temple in the 1940s and '50s when he was played by Kim Peacock, and the role of the great detective's wife was taken by another prolific radio veteran, Marjorie Westbury. The popular theme tune which introduced each episode of the serial was originally from Rimsky-Korsakov's *Scheherazade*, and later from Vivian Ellis's *Coronation Scot*.

Years later Durbridge said he was sorry to hear about the demolition of Kirkgate Market and Swan Arcade when he came to stay with his friends, the Greenwood family, who were Bradford and Leeds clothiers.

Other books and plays, especially thrillers, were a mark of his prolific pen throughout his life, but perhaps he will mostly be remembered for the Paul Temple radio and television series. Francis Durbridge died at his home in Walton-on-Thames in 1998 at the age of eighty-six.

John Duttine

Actor

To play John the Disciple in *Jesus of Nazareth*, and to feature in the credits with such illustrious actors as Lord Olivier, Sir Ralph Richardson, James Mason, Rod Steiger, Anne Bancroft, Christopher Plummer, Michael York and Robert Powell, 27-year-old John Duttine had come a long way from Buttershaw Comprehensive School.

John was born in Barnsley in 1949, the youngest of five boys. On the death of his father in 1953 the family moved to Bradford, where his grandmother Elsie Hampton lived in Horton Bank Top. He attended Ryan Street Junior School, later Buttershaw Comprehensive, where he first became aware of the theatre, encouraged by his drama teacher, Janet Beard.

By the time he left school he had already played Macbeth and Hamlet in school productions, and Mark Antony for the newly formed West Riding Youth Theatre. As well as attending classes at Bradford Civic Theatre, John successfully auditioned for the Drama Centre in London. After three years of rigorous training under the auspices of John Blatchley and Christopher Fettes, John gained access to the newly formed, and later to become famous, Glasgow Citizens' Theatre in 1970, where he played numerous roles over a two-year period.

He spent the early 1970s in various repertory theatres including Watford Palace and the Nottingham Playhouse. His first TV appearance was alongside Francesca Annis in the BBC's production of *A Pin to See the Peepshow*, a four-part series about the notorious trial, conviction and subsequent hanging of Edith Thompson and Freddy Bywaters of the early 1920s.

This led to many roles on TV including *Softly Softly*, *Z Cars*, *Warship*, and in 1976 as John the Disciple in Franco Zeffirelli's *Jesus of Nazareth*. After filming for six months in North Africa, he returned to the UK and won the role of Keith Nicholson in Jack Rosenthal's *Spend, Spend, Spend*, about the Yorkshire couple Keith and Viv Nicholson who famously won the pools in the early 1960s and notoriously spent the lot! There followed more TV appearances, including the first adaptation of a Catherine Cookson novel, *The Mallens*. He achieved his ambition in 1978 by working with his hero Laurence Olivier in a production of *Saturday, Sunday, Monday* for Granada TV. In 1979 he landed the part of David Powlett-Jones in R.F. Delderfield's *To Serve Them All My Days*, a thirteen-part series about a Welsh teacher in an English public school. This won him a *TV Times* Best Actor award. More TV was to follow: *The Devil's Crown*, *The Day of the Triffids*, the US mini-series, *A Woman of Substance*, filmed partly in North Yorkshire, *Lame Ducks*, a BBC sitcom, and his first film, *Who Dares Wins*. In 1989 he landed the role of 'The Actor', alongside Charles Kay, in Susan Hill's *The Woman in Black* which opened at the Lyric, Hammersmith. It was a return to the stage after many years. The play was hugely successful and moved to the West End in 1990, and continues to thrive at the Fortune Theatre today.

More theatre followed, including another Mark Antony in *Julius Caesar*, and *Richard II*. In 1992 John played the lead role in Ruth Rendell's *Talking to Strange Men*, where he first met his wife Mel Martin. A Middle and Far East tour of Bernard Slade's *Same Time Next Year* with Mel followed, and a further production of *A Woman in Black* at the Olympic Theatre in Dublin. In 1996 this production was taken to Charleston, South Carolina, for the Spoletto Festival, a prestigious gathering of theatre, music and arts.

In 1997 John and Mel Martin upped sticks and moved to Cornwall where they now live in a seventeenth-century farmhouse which they are slowly and painstakingly restoring. Duttine's recent TV appearances have been in *The Hunt for the Yorkshire Ripper*, and most recently he and Mel appeared together as defending and prosecuting council in the trial of Little Mo in the BBC's *EastEnders*.

With over thirty-five years of acting behind him, John has many more years of commanding performances to come.

Adrian Edmondson

Actor, Writer and Comedian

It is hard to define the career of Adrian Edmondson because he has so many strings to his bow: director, writer, actor, comedian, and he has been successful in all.

Adrian was born on 21 January 1957 at 58 Plumpton Gardens, Wrose. His father was deputy head at Drummond Middle School. Adrian attended Swain House Junior School, and Hutton Junior School after the family moved to Doctor Hill on Highfield Road, opposite the fire station.

Most of Adrian's relatives were in the woollen industry, selling from a stall in Kirkgate Market, and buying wool from the large warehouse in Vicar Lane. Adrian quite often worked on the Bradford stall, but preferred travelling around with his uncle and granddad to Dewsbury, Doncaster and Sheffield, selling cloth on the market stalls. Occasionally he worked at a warehouse for another uncle, building up an impressive stamp collection from the huge number of sample packages from all over the world, in his holidays from Pocklington Boarding School.

From Pocklington he went to Manchester University in 1975 to study drama. There he met Rik Mayall and joined him in the comedy troupe 20th Century Coyote. After graduation, the group split up, leaving Adrian and Rik as a double act, touring Britain with various two-man shows until they joined a number of talented artists then appearing at London's Comedy Store. In the late 1980s Adrian co-founded the Comic Strip Club, subsequently playing leading parts in all the episodes of *The Comic Strip Presents*. He went on to play Vyvyan in BBC TV's hugely successful *The Young Ones*, also starring Rik Mayall, whom he later joined in writing and performing.

He starred in two television films devised by Les Blair, *Honest, Decent and True* and *Newshounds*, winner of the 1990 BAFTA for the best single drama. In the same year, with Rik Mayall, he created the award-winning *Bottom*, their most popular sitcom to date. This also became a hit stage show. Edmondson's other television works include *If You See God, Tell Him*, and guest roles in such hits as *Blackadder* and *Absolutely Fabulous* (written by, and starring, his wife Jennifer Saunders). On stage he has starred in West End productions of *The Rocky Horror Show* and W*aiting for Godot* (with Rik Mayall).

He played at St George's Hall, Bradford, with his spoof rock band Bad News in the late 1980s. They played there again in the 1990s on the *Bottom* tour, and at one point he mentioned to the audience that Bradford was his home town – the roar was out of this world!

Adrian has a distinctive brand of humour, some say in the old tradition. Now a self-made millionaire he still holds great affection for Bradford, even after being badly beaten up outside Sunwin House in his teens: how's that for loyalty to the city?

Frederick William Eurich

Bacteriologist

Anthrax is little heard of today. However, in the nineteenth and early twentieth centuries it was the scourge of industrial workers in the Bradford wool trade, especially the wool sorters. The name of one man stands out above all others in the fight against this disease – Frederick William Eurich.

He was born in Chemnitz, Germany, in 1869. His father was in the yarn trade, and the company he worked for had a branch in Bradford, so it was in 1874 that the family moved to 7 Selborne Villas in the city. Many other families emigrated from Germany and settled in Bradford towards the end of the nineteenth century. They brought with them a wealth of interest in music and the arts that had a significant effect on the cultural life of the city they adopted.

Frederick went to a local preparatory school, Mrs Featherstone's in Manningham, for four terms, then aged nine to Bradford Grammar School. While at the school he fell seriously ill with scarlet fever and was admitted to Bradford Fever Hospital, where conditions were so appalling that he took a long time to recover. Perhaps because of this experience of illness and hospital, he lost interest in Classics and determined to become a doctor, studying first at Edinburgh University and then Edinburgh Medical School in 1886. After qualifying, he undertook postgraduate research in Germany, and then obtained a position as physician at Lancashire County Asylum.

He began to practise in Bradford in 1896, and set up a general practice at 65 Manningham Lane. Over the years Dr Eurich held various posts in Bradford and these gradually took him into the work that he really wanted to do, medical research.

In 1901 he was appointed bacteriologist to the city of Bradford and to the Bradford Anthrax Investigation Board. He had a laboratory at 22 Edmund Street, where he carried out his many investigations on wool and hairs, at considerable danger to himself. Alpaca and mohair had been coming into the West Riding since 1847 and the deaths among people handling these fibres were causing increasing concern. Many attacks were fatal within a few days; sometimes a man would go home from the mill feeling out of sorts and would be dead in 15–20 hours. A sorter giving evidence at an inquest said he personally knew twenty-two men who had died after sorting mohair. The nature of wool-sorter's disease was not understood, and even after it was diagnosed its complete elimination baffled the industry for thirty-five years.

Eurich led the investigations, realising that humans contracted the illness after coming into contact with the blood of infected animals. After years of experiment and the examination of over 12,000 samples, a scheme was adopted under which all dangerous wool was directed to one port – Liverpool. Here a disinfection station was erected to sterilise the wool, a measure that undoubtedly reduced the number of anthrax cases. It was augmented by a set of rigorous precautions which enabled

workers with knowledge to spot any likely contaminated material in the various mills. These precautions remained in force throughout the woollen industry's heyday.

For many years Dr Eurich was also professor of forensic medicine at Leeds University and an honorary physician at the Bradford Royal Infirmary and the Eye and Ear Hospital. At the infirmary he had a Saturday morning surgery which was 'free of charge'. He was also pathologist to Bradford Corporation for some years.

In recognition of his work Dr Eurich was awarded a special gold medal by the Textile Institute in 1937. He was the first non-member ever to receive this award. When the presentation was made a speaker said that Eurich's work was to the wool trade what Davy's safety lamp was to the mining industry.

Not very long after this Dr Eurich retired to Ilkley, then to the New Forest where he died at his son's home at Dibden Purlieu, Hampshire, in February 1945.

Richard Eurich OBE

Artist

Richard Eurich caught the terrible beauty of war in his work, distilling the awful truth that battles of human life and death often take place on beautiful days in beautiful places.

Richard Ernst Eurich was born at 7 Lindum Terrace, Manningham, on 14 March 1903. His German-born father was Dr F.W. Eurich, professor of forensic medicine and bacteriologist, famous for his work on the eradication of anthrax. Richard was educated at St George's School, Harpenden, and from 1918 to 1921 at Bradford Grammar School. From there he went on to the Bradford School of Arts and Crafts. After two years he progressed to the famous Slade School of Art in London. He won seven prizes for drawing and composition at the Slade.

With the encouragement of Eric Gill and Sir Edward Marsh he had his first one-man exhibition of pencil drawings at the Goupil Galleries in 1929. He was a consummate master of coastscapes and beachscapes, with a wonderful eye for details of shifting light and the strange perspective that these provide. In this, he was close to his hero Turner. His oil paintings were seen from time to time at the New English Art Club, and in 1933 he had the first of sixteen exhibitions at the Redfearn Gallery, which included *Bathers on the Beach* and *Cargo Boats on the Solent*. In 1937 he exhibited at the Royal Academy for the first time and in 1938 he showed thirty-five paintings of Cornish harbours at Redfearns.

When the withdrawal from Dunkirk took place in June 1940, he immediately realised that the subject merited epic treatment. He wrote to the War Artists' Committee. After discreet testing of his abilities, he was seconded in 1941 to the Royal Navy and given an honorary commission as a captain in the Royal Marines as a war artist. His *Dunkirk Beach May 1940* was exhibited at the Royal Academy in 1941 and was purchased by the Canadian War Museum. After the war Winston Churchill declared it was the finest painting of the war years.

The Imperial War Museum purchased the *Great Convoy to North Africa*, the Maritime Museum secured *Withdrawal from Dunkirk* and the Tate Gallery acquired *Survivors of a Torpedoed Ship*, based on a true incident. There were many other more complex paintings of convoys and air raids.

After the war he taught at Camberwell School of Art until 1967 and in 1984 was awarded the OBE. This was followed in 1989 by an doctorate from Bradford University. In 1991 his paintings were exhibited at the Imperial War Museum.

Richard Eurich died in Southampton on 6 June 1992 aged eighty-nine. His ashes were scattered at Lepe beach, Hampshire, where he found the inspiration for so many of his pictures.

Vic Feather
Trade Unionist

Vic Feather was born on 10 April 1908 at 9 Malvern Street, off Leeds Road, Bradford, the house being typical of the long cramped stone back-to-back terraces built in the nineteenth century. His father, Harry Feather, was a socialist of such deep conviction that he called his second son Victor Grayson Hardie after two of the heroes of Labour's early parliamentary battles.

The family moved to Ripon Street, Otley Road, where Victor lived until he was twenty-two. His early education was at Undercliffe School, followed by Hanson Grammar School. He was fifteen years old and still wearing short pants when he left the Grammar School to start work with the Bradford Co-op at 12s 6d a week as a delivery boy. He also drew illustrations for the *Bradford Pioneer*, the weekly paper run by Barbara Castle's father Frank Betts.

Vic immediately joined the shop workers' union and became the office subscription collector. Within five years he was chairman of the branch of the former National Union of Distributive and Allied Workers, and at twenty-one was a delegate to Bradford Trades Council. On the death of his father the family had moved from Ripon Street, Undercliffe, to the Ravenscliffe council estate.

He was known as quite a soap-box orator, to whom you went with your troubles, and he spent many weekends on Shipley Glen practising his public speaking, realising he would need skill in the speaking arts if he were ever to realise his ambition of eyeball-to-eyeball encounters with politicians.

In 1937 he joined the staff of the Trades Union Congress, beating 350 applicants for the post. His political and trade union toughness was well known and he endeared himself to all political parties. Part of his human toughness was shown during the Second World War when he was serving as an ARP warden in London. In 1941 he received a War Office Citation for his part in the rescue of a youth from his bomb-damaged home.

In 1947 he became Assistant General Secretary of the TUC, and its leader in 1970. He retired in 1974 and was made a life peer. Vic Feather died at the age of sixty-eight on 28 July 1976.

Peter Firth

Actor

Peter Firth is best known for his film and stage portrayal of Alan Strang in Peter Shaffer's *Equus*, a role that earned him a 1974 Golden Globe for Best Supporting Actor, an Academy Award nomination, a Tony Award nomination, the Theatre World Award and the Plays and Players Award for Best Young Actor. He is now an international star.

Born on 27 October 1953 in Chapel Street, Eccleshill, he attended Hutton School and later Hanson Boys Grammar School. His desire to be an actor developed early, and aged fourteen he attended classes at the Bradford Civic Theatre. Such was his progress that he was recommended to Yorkshire Television and got a part in the *The Flaxton Boys* (1971–2) before progressing to the stage and screen. He made a brief appearance in Franco Zeffirelli's *Brother Son, Sister Moon* (1973) in the same year that he created his acclaimed stage role in *Equus*. He spent the 1974 season with the National Theatre Company appearing in *Spring Awakening*, *Measure for Measure* and *Romeo and Juliet*.

In 1976 he had his first major film role as a novice First World War fighter pilot in *Aces High*. He followed this with the title role in Tony Richardson's *Joseph Andrews* (1977). After his Oscar-nominated turn in *Equus*, he played yet another troubled youth in *When You Comin' Back, Red Ryder?* (1979) before returning to period drama as the cleric's son who marries and abandons *Tess* (1979).

In 1985 he was cast in *Letter to Brezhnev*, in which he played a Russian sailor romancing a Liverpudlian girl. He spoke Russian again as the doomed sailor Avan Putin in John McTiernan's *The Hunt for Red October* (1990). He was also a sympathetic doctor treating Joy Gresham (Debra Winger) in Richard Attenborough's *Shadowlands* (1992), and excelled as the nasty stage manager in Mike Newell's *An Awfully Big Adventure* (1995). Peter Firth returned to British TV in 1994 to star in the weekly series *Heartbeat*.

His recent films include *Chill Factor* (1999) as the revenge-seeking Major Andrew Brynner, and the 2001 epic *Pearl Harbor*, as captain of the *West Virginia*.

W.E. Forster

Member of Parliament

On 17 May 1890 there was great rejoicing in Bradford – flags flew everywhere and special peals were rung on the bells of the town hall and the parish church. It was on this day that the statue of William Edward Forster was unveiled in the newly named Forster Square. For twenty-five years he was one of the Members of Parliament for the Borough of Bradford. He was also the father of universal elementary education and instigator of the 1870 Education Act.

Born 11 July 1818 at Bradpole, Dorset, it was in 1841, as the result of a conversation in a stagecoach, that Forster moved to Bradford to engage in the wool industry. The following year he joined William Fison in partnership in a woollen manufacturing business at Waterloo Mills, Market Street, in the centre of Bradford (on the site later occupied by the Swan Arcade). The business later moved to a larger establishment in the Manchester Road area.

In 1850, with his partner, he bought two cotton mills in Burley-in-Wharfedale called Greenholme Mills, with the intention of converting them for worsted manufacturing. The mill became a thriving establishment and the number employed there rose in ten years from 300 to 500.

Although elected MP for Bradford in 1861, Forster still concentrated his attention on local interests, especially his workforce. Working hours were long, 12 hours for men and 10 for women and young people. He organised reading rooms, evening classes and half-time education for children aged eight to fifteen. Entertainments were provided on several occasions and what must have been one of the first works trips ever was the company excursion to London in 1862. On that occasion, between 500 and 600 workers were taken to London for two days, staying at the newly opened Cook's Hostel in Brompton, which was so new that the furniture and people arrived at the same time. The railway had not yet reached Burley-in-Wharfedale, so the whole venture began and ended with a long procession to and from Apperley Bridge station.

During his first year as an MP, Forster took an active part in the struggle that eventually led to the second Reform act. This Act, which recognised the right of most working men to a parliamentary vote, had his full support. In Gladstone's government in 1868 Forster became Vice-President of the Council. In this post he was given the task of providing some form of education for the hordes of children in the industrial towns who were not catered for in any way by the existing schools. His Education Act of 1870 saw the introduction of school boards whose job it was to see that there were enough school places for all the children in the district. The struggle over the Education Act was an agonising one for Forster, but he had to cope with even more complex problems towards the end of his life in his position as Chief Secretary for Ireland in Gladstone's second government. He was a hated representative of British rule in Ireland, and his well-intentioned schemes for relief in famine areas did nothing to gain the sympathy of men who were determined, above all else, to gain Home Rule. Various threats were made against

his life and in April 1882, a chance alteration in his travelling plans saved him from a well-organised assassination plot.

Burley-in-Wharfedale saw very little of him during these years as he spent a great deal of his time in Dublin and London. He remained active in politics until the late summer of 1885. Throughout the following winter he was ill and died on 5 April at his London home. After an elaborate ceremony in Westminster Abbey his body (in accordance with his wishes) was taken to Burley-in-Wharfedale, where on 10 April 1886 he was interred at 'God's Little Acre'.

Trevor Foster MBE

Bradford Northern and Great Britain Rugby Player

Trevor Foster, a tall, athletically built man from the Welsh valleys, soon adapted his style from the union to the league code, and became one of the best forwards that Bradford Northern ever had. Later he became one of Bradford's leading and best-loved citizens.

Born in 1914, Trevor Forster was the youngest of six at his parents' public house, The Church House, in Newport. His school, from the juniors upwards, was Holy Cross RC. His early rugby union career was at this school and it was through the parish priest, Father Honon, that he began to develop as a wing-forward. He was soon playing for Newport schoolboys.

Having left school at fourteen, he joined the Pill Harriers nursery team in the Gwent League, during which time he worked at the family public house where his father was losing his sight. Soon he was in the Newport national team. Word of his talent soon reached the northern rugby league clubs and he was approached during his first full season with Newport (1937/8) by Wigan. He refused, as his ambition was to play for Wales; however, when Dai Rees, the manager of Bradford Northern, paid him a visit he accepted, and signed in September 1938 for £400. There is no doubt he would have had many Welsh caps but for his decision to move north.

After a few weeks adjusting from union to league, he soon found a regular place in the side, making 24 appearances during the 1938/9 season and scoring 11 tries and a goal, his first try coming in his second match on 12 November 1938 against Oldham.

During the war Trevor was conscripted, joining the King's Own Yorkshire Light Infantry. He was promoted to staff sergeant instructor with the Physical Training Corps, during which time he played some of the wartime league matches for Northern. In 1945 he was in Egypt, and in 1946 went on the first rugby league tour to Australia and New Zealand since 1936.

Trevor will be remembered by most as a key figure in the great Bradford Northern side that reached successive Wembley finals in 1947, 1948 and 1949. He scored the crucial try in the 1947 victory over Leeds. Northern bounced back after the disappointing defeat against Wigan the following year and notched up another victory in 1949 to sink Halifax 12–0.

With a total of 433 matches played, one goal, 133 tries, 392 points, 3 Great Britain caps, and the Great Britain Tour in 1946, Trevor played his last match at Wakefield on 20 April 1955. Despite retirement, Trevor continued to serve Bradford and was Rees's assistant between March and December 1960. A seat on the board followed and in recent years he has been the club's official time-keeper for all first team matches.

Noted as the charities champion, Trevor is involved in Bradford Police Club for Young People, Cancer Support Centres, Friends of Bradford Royal Infirmary, CHAS Housing Aid Centre, the Bradford Society for Mentally Handicapped Children, St Cuthbert's RC Church, St Vincent de Paul Society, and drug awareness campaigns.

Many honours have followed: in 2001 he was awarded an MBE, in July 2002 July he received an honorary doctorate from Bradford University and in November 2002 a road in Odsal was named Trevor Foster Way.

Anyone who has had the pleasure of knowing and talking to Trevor Foster cannot have failed to notice the warm and very likeable manner of the man. He is without doubt one of the city's greatest ambassadors, a true caring gentleman.

Gareth Gates

Pop Star

The youngest and most recent Bradford celebrity, Gareth Gates shot to fame through the ITV series *Pop Idol*.

Gareth was born at St Luke's Hospital on 12 July 1984. He is the eldest child of Paul and Wendy Gates. His father was an engineer, later a postman, his mother a housewife and foster carer. The family lived in a flat in East Bowling, but later moved to Liley Street in the same area. Gareth attended Lowerfield Middle School in East Bowling.

Gareth suffered from a speech disability, as did his father. He found the best way to express himself and say the things he always wanted to say was through the power of song. Gareth was first noticed for his singing ability by a teacher at the age of eight. He joined the Bradford Cathedral Church Choir where his talent was developed. By the time he was fifteen, he knew singing was to be his career. In February 1999 he appeared on *Steps to the Stars*.

In summer 2001 Gareth auditioned in Manchester for *Pop Idol*, the programme on the lookout for a solo act to take the music industry by storm. In front of a judging panel of Simon Cowell, Nicki Chapman, Pete Waterman and Dr Fox, Gareth gave a breathtaking rendition of 'Flying without Wings' and immediately got through the first round. At the London heats Gareth went through to the final fifty. TV viewers gave him an astounding 62 per cent of the votes when he sang 'Flying without Wings' again on the first live show.

The final ten proved to be a challenge, with very tough competition. The final four contestants were Gareth, Darius, Will and Zoë. Extremely polished versions of 'Unchained Melody' and 'Yesterday' led to Gareth's being cast in the final against 23-year-old Will Young. Over eight and a half million people phoned in to vote, and the results could not have been closer. Gareth got a staggering total of over four million votes, yet ended up in second place, just beaten by Will. However, he and Will had already both been signed by Simon Fuller at 19 Management and told that, whoever won, they would both have a career.

Gareth, who is certainly determined and hard-working, released 'Unchained Melody' weeks after the final of *Pop Idol* and immediately knocked Will off the UK number one slot. Several weeks later it was still the most popular song around.

Gareth has continually given interviews and speeches, coping admirably with his stammer and proving he can handle any situation.

Harry Gration

Television Presenter

Harry Gration's reputation as a sports reporter has taken him all over the world. His is a familiar face which is known to millions. He is a professional and very proud of the city of his birth.

Born in October 1950 at Southfield Lane, Great Horton, he later moved to Toller Lane. He attended St Philip's School in Girlington, where he was also a choirboy. His father was the manager of Boots the Chemist in Darley Street, and his grandfather a tram driver, a fact of which Harry is proud.

Some of his happiest memories are of his days in Toller Lane playing cricket and football in the street. The family later moved to Little Horton Lane where his mother had a share in a dress shop (which is still there today), living above the shop and handy for his father to play snooker in the club next door.

Initially a Park Avenue fan, he moved to favour Bradford City as he grew older. Or was it something to do with Avenue going out of existence? He attended Leeds Grammar School and later St Peter's, York. In 1969 he was at St John's Teacher Training College at York, and then in 1973 he taught history at Rodillian School, Rothwell. In 1971 he began freelance radio sportscasting after persuading Radio Leeds to let him commentate on rugby league matches. For a while he did sports commentaries in the evenings and taught during the day.

In 1979 when Radio Leeds offered him a three-month contract as Sports Editor, he took a chance and gave up his job. He never looked back. In 1982 he joined *Look North* which he presented with Judith Stamper. Harry had embarked on a successful career in broadcasting that has seen him work on BBC radio, both locally and nationally, and in programmes such as *Match of the Day*, *Grandstand*, *Sportsnight*, and *South Today*.

In 1994 he left *Look North* to work for the Rugby League as their Public Affairs Executive, before returning to broadcasting a year later. He also worked for BBC's Olympic and Commonwealth coverage in Sydney 2000 where he commentated on judo and taekwondo. Harry has won two Royal Television Society Awards for his sports documentaries, *White Rose in Africa* (1992) and *Dickie Bird, a Rare Species* (1997).

In 1999 he returned to *Look North* after a five-year break and is a great favourite with the viewers alongside Bradford-born Christa Ackroyd.

Carl Gresham

Impresario and Agent

Carl Gresham began his career as a broadcaster, but soon ventured into employment as a columnist, disc jockey, actor, presenter and TV/film agent. While fulfilling these roles it was perhaps inevitable that he should develop personal friendships with many of the stars he later employed when he launched his 'Personal Appearance' promotions at bingo halls, galas and discos.

Carl was born in Bradford, the family living at 13 Runswick Grove, Bankfoot. For many years the road was known as 'Celebrity Grove' because all Carl's friends from *Coronation Street* came for tea, the host being Carl's beloved mother. His father had died years previously. Those included were Pat Phoenix (Elsie Tanner), Doris Speed (Annie Walker), Margot Bryant (Minnie Caldwell), Violet Carson (Ena Sharples), Bernard Youens (Stan Ogden – Carl later became his personal manager) and many more. All shared tea (or a noggin or two) at Greshland House.

Not all his earlier career moves were meticulously planned! After he was sacked by his local record shop for taking the job as stand-in for Tom Courtenay in the film *Billy Liar*, the *Telegraph & Argus* showbiz guru Peter Holdsworth suggested he did a story about the local lad doing well. Courtenay told Carl that if the story appeared in the paper he'd be sacked from the film! It made page one and Carl was sacked. Years later Carl bumped into Tom in Regent Street and reminded him of the occasion. Tom remembered it well and made a general comment that whatever happened all those years ago, Gresh had certainly made his name in the business.

Following his sacking from *Billy Liar* Carl went on to other ventures, and if you look very closely at early *Coronation Street* episodes you might just catch a glimpse of him when he played Jerry Booth's cycling club mate.

To earn extra cash he joined the list of many TV companies' extras and found himself working in major television studios throughout the north, particularly Granada. This gave him the opportunity to meet up with many of the stars who were later to work through his promotional and management company. These included Morecambe and Wise, Pat Phoenix, Patrick Mower, Peter Wyngarde, Gordon Jackson, Frazer Hines, Dennis Waterman and international star Tony Curtis.

Carl launched his exclusive 'Celebrity Personal Appearance' agency which arranged everything from the booking of the stars to the production of posters. He recalls one occasion when Woolworth's booked thirty-six celebrities to appear in thirty-six different stores throughout the UK, all on one day. 'I had to dig deep for that job', said Carl. 'Where on earth would I find so many star names at one time?' – but he managed it.

The entertainment world ranks high among Carl's clients. At one time he supplied presentation gifts for programmes like Yorkshire's *Countdown* and Tyne Tees' *Cross Wits*. He has also supplied specialist merchandise to arenas, theatres and concert performers. Carl was the first person to introduce the huge foam 'boo

hands', as seen on TV's *Gladiators* and at pantomimes. He also imports and supplies, quite literally, tons of the flashing goodies you see at both indoor and outdoor events.

In 2003 Carl arranged special promotional showings of the film *Calendar Girls* involving the original 'Calendar Girls' from the Rylstone Institute, Skipton, and members of the film cast. The first of these took place at the Palace Theatre, Newark.

He is currently planning publication of *The Truth, the Whole Truth and Nothing but the Truth*, a book about his many show business friends, a book of interviews and anecdotes from over 200 stars of screen, television and theatre, warts and all. Carl's knowledge of showbusiness and the stars has no bounds. He is on first-name terms with most of those we only read about, and they consider him a trustworthy, reliable and thoroughly professional friend.

Barry Hanson

Film and Television Producer

Barry Hanson's CV is a lengthy volume, stretching from the late 1960s to the present day. He was born on 10 August 1943 when his family lived at 340 Kings Road on Bradford's Swain House estate. He attended Swain House Junior School and later Belle Vue Grammar School. He joined the Bradford Cathedral Boys' Brigade as a drummer.

When the Bradford Civic Playhouse wanted drummers to play in *Hamlet and the King*, he volunteered and, in his own words, 'was smitten'. He became a member of the Group Theatre (an offshoot from the Playhouse). On leaving school he went to Newcastle University to study English. Later he studied theatre, working in and around the country and gaining a detailed knowledge of theatre life, particularly production.

In 1967 he was appointed Assistant Director of the Royal Court Theatre, London, where he directed many plays. With this experience, in 1972 he became Drama Script Editor, Producer and Director in the newly opened Pebble Mill TV studios in Birmingham. From 1975 he produced films and plays for Jeremy Isaacs and Verity Lambert at Thames TV, including *The Naked Civil Servant* with John Hurt, directed by Jack Gold, which won the Prix Italia, Bafta and the International Emmy for best drama. This was followed by the six-part thriller *Out* starring Tom Bell.

In 1979 Barry joined ITC, the movie-making subsidiary of Lord Grade's ATV, to produce films including *Bloody Kids*, John Osborne's *Very Like a Whale* with Alan Bates, and the classic *The Long Good Friday*, which gave Bob Hoskins his first starring major movie role. In 1982 he was a producer for Goldcrest Films and TV while founding Telekation International, which produced educational series and drama for Channel 4, including *The Wine Programme* and *Everybody Here* (Britain's first multicultural children's series).

From 1987–9 he was Senior Drama Producer for BBC single films, and in 1989 Head of Drama BBC Birmingham, responsible for all regional drama output including the long-running series *Kinsey*, and *Lady Chatterley's Lover*, directed by Ken Russell. From 1994 he was Head of Production for London Films, producing *Resort to Murder* for BBC1 and also setting up the serial *The Scarlet Pimpernel*.

Today he is Consultant Storyliner for Channel 5, a consultant for Moonstone International – judging, screenwriting and interviewing candidates for the writers' and directors' labs – and a consultant for Dan Films for feature film projects. He is currently working on a critical biography of Alan Bleasdale.

Barbara Jane Harrison GC
Air Stewardess

Three women were awarded the George Cross for service with the Resistance in the Second World War. The fourth ever presented to a woman was the first award to a female civilian and it was made posthumously to Miss Harrison for her gallantry at Heathrow Airport, London on 8 April 1968.

Barbara Jane Harrison was born at the family home, 2 Kingsdale Crescent, Bolton Road, Bradford, on 24 May 1945. She attended Greystones Preparatory School, Pollard Lane, before moving to Scarborough with her family in 1956. She first worked in Martins Bank in Doncaster then went to California to be an au pair. On her return to Britain Jane became an air stewardess with the British Overseas Airways Corporation (now part of British Airways).

On 8 April 1968, soon after taking off from Heathrow Airport, the number two engine of her BOAC Boeing 707 caught fire and fell from the aircraft, leaving a fierce fire burning at the engine position. A few minutes later the aircraft made an emergency landing at the airport where the fire on the port wing intensified. One of Miss Harrison's duties in an emergency was to help the steward at the rear station open up escape routes for passengers. When they landed, Miss Harrison and the steward opened the rear gallery door and inflated the chute, which became twisted on the way down. The steward had to climb down to straighten it before it could be used and once out of the aircraft he was unable to return. This left Miss Harrison alone to help the passengers out of the aircraft. With flames and explosions all around her she encouraged some to jump from the aircraft and tried to push others out. At this stage escape from the tail of the plane became impossible and she directed her passengers to another exit while she remained at her post. She was finally overcome while trying to save an elderly couple who were seated in one of the last rows and whose bodies were found close to that of the Miss Harrison's. The *London Gazette* of 8 August 1968 cited the posthumous GC award.

She was a remarkable girl, who helped save the lives of the crew and 121 passengers. Only six people died in the tragedy. There is a plaque dedicated to Miss Harrison at St Lawrence's C of E Church, Scawby, Scarborough. Her George Cross was sold in 1987 and is on display in the crew's quarters at Heathrow. There is also a plaque in her memory in the airport chapel. In the year 2000 she was commemorated in the Memorial Gallery at Bradford's City Hall along with other local recipients of bravery medals.

Steven Hartley
Actor

Steven Hartley is the actor with the rich, articulate voice, who was so convincing as Superintendent Tom Chandler in the TV series *The Bill* that when he took part in the London Marathon he was jeered along the route!

Steven was born at Shipley Maternity Hospital on 12 August 1960. The family lived at 22a Bingley Road, Shipley, above a butcher's shop, later moving to a small house in Fern Hill Road, Saltaire, while his father Michael did his National Service. His mother Maureen worked at Fairfield Nurseries on Shipley Glen, and when his father returned they moved to 30 Norwood Avenue, Shipley.

In 1965 the family moved to Croydon, although Steven spent a lot of time travelling back and forth to family gatherings at Wensley Avenue, Shipley. His father worked for the RSPCA, which involved many moves around the country, but the family eventually settled in York. After leaving school, Steven found success as an amateur boxer in the county.

Steven spent two years in advertising for the *Yorkshire Evening Press* before moving to London in 1981 where he studied at the London Academy of Music and Dramatic Art. Following graduation in 1984 he played in rep at various theatres including the Bradford Alhambra (in the musical *Babes in Arms* with Matthew Kelly and Su Pollard).

His first film was *Young Toscanini* directed by Franco Zeffirelli and starring Elizabeth Taylor. Steven played the bad guy, Heckler. His other films include *Columbus* alongside Marlon Brando, Tom Selleck and Catherine Zeta Jones. In 1989 he spent some time in Los Angeles before returning home to do more theatre, including *An Evening with Gary Lineker* in the West End.

Three months were spent in Russia filming *The Final Warning*, about the Chernobyl disaster, in which he played the real-life character Alex Mashenko. He followed this up with the role of Fostor in the film *Split Second* with Rutger Hauer.

In 1987 Steven played Matthew Jackson in *EastEnders*. He had meetings with United Artists to replace Roger Moore in the Bond series as 007, but the part went to Timothy Dalton, Steven 'thinks he was too young then [and now he's] too old!'

Other TV series in which he has appeared include *Press Gang, The Young Indiana Jones Chronicles* (USA), *Sharman, Pie in the Sky, Married with Children* (USA), *Out of Order, Bad Boys, The Governor, Trial and Retribution, Where the Heart Is*, Tom Chandler in *The Bill* of course, and recently as Dr Marcus Denby in *Holby City*.

Steven is also in great demand for TV and radio voiceovers. His most recent theatre role was in the award-winning production of *Oliver*, playing Bill Sykes alongside Russ Abbott and Robert Lindsay.

Denis Healey

Politician

Once described as 'more like a hearty schoolmaster or a yeoman farmer than a politician', the man with the well-known bushy eyebrows held two of government's top offices: Secretary of State for Defence and Chancellor of the Exchequer.

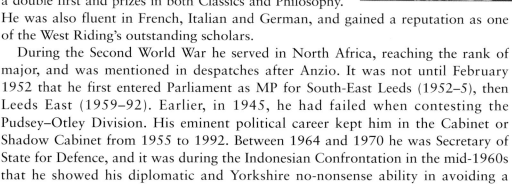

Denis Winston Healey was born in Kent on 30 August 1917. When he was five, the family moved from Woolwich to Holker Street, Keighley, and later to Back Lane, Riddlesden. His father was employed as Principal of Keighley Technical College. Denis attended Keighley Girls' Grammar School – which then included a mixed junior department.

He won a scholarship to Bradford Grammar School and went on to Balliol College, Oxford, where he gained a double first and prizes in both Classics and Philosophy. He was also fluent in French, Italian and German, and gained a reputation as one of the West Riding's outstanding scholars.

During the Second World War he served in North Africa, reaching the rank of major, and was mentioned in despatches after Anzio. It was not until February 1952 that he first entered Parliament as MP for South-East Leeds (1952–5), then Leeds East (1959–92). Earlier, in 1945, he had failed when contesting the Pudsey–Otley Division. His eminent political career kept him in the Cabinet or Shadow Cabinet from 1955 to 1992. Between 1964 and 1970 he was Secretary of State for Defence, and it was during the Indonesian Confrontation in the mid-1960s that he showed his diplomatic and Yorkshire no-nonsense ability in avoiding a situation comparable to Vietnam.

From 1974 to 1979 he was Chancellor of the Exchequer, and from 1980 to 1983 Deputy Leader of the Labour Party. In 1992 he stood down from his parliamentary seat of Leeds East, and after forty-seven years in politics he was made a life peer, taking the title from his childhood days spent at Riddlesden: Lord Healey of Riddlesden in the County of York.

Among his many honours and awards he was made a D.Litt at Bradford University in 1983, and a Freeman of Leeds in 1992. In retirement he has turned back towards his roots by becoming President of the National Trust's Yorkshire Moors and Dales Appeal. His love of Yorkshire shines through in his autobiography, 'Every Whitsun we had our school camp in a field by the Wharfe near Appletreewick. . . . One day was always set aside for a walk down the river through Bolton Woods to the ruined Abbey, then up the Valley of Desolation and over the moors to Simon's Seat, before dropping back into the valley to camp. This part of Wharfedale is for me what Shropshire was for Housman, "the land of lost content".'

James Douglas Hill DFC
Film Director and Screen Writer

In 1966 *Born Free* starring Virginia McKenna and Bill Travers hit the silver screen. Adapted from a book by Joy Adamson, it went on to win two Oscars, and it was directed by Bradford's James D. Hill.

James Douglas Hill was born in Eldwick near Bingley in 1919, the family later moving to Duchy Avenue, Heaton. He was educated at Belle Vue School, and an essay he wrote on film was successful in bringing him a scholarship to the London Film School. While at this school he made a short educational film, then embarked on a cine-photography course. During this time he made short comedy skit films, one of which was shot on the outskirts of Bradford during a vacation and was shown to audiences at the Bradford Civic Playhouse.

He joined the documentary unit of the GPO Film Unit as assistant director but when the Second World War came he volunteered for the RAF and was commissioned as an air observer, subsequently joining the RAF film unit.

From 1940 onwards he flew numerous day and night missions, taking part in raids over continental Europe, including Berlin – the action scenes he filmed can still be seen in wartime newsreels. One raid was on a factory in Eindhoven, Holland, on 6 December 1942. His aircraft was a Mosquito, which was the only one used on that raid strictly for photographic purposes, the other aircraft being target markers. This daylight raid resulted in casualties of no less than 15 per cent. For this and previous actions he was awarded the Distinguished Flying Cross, and this is recorded in the *London Gazette* of 28 March 1944.

Later in the war he was shot down, taken prisoner and interned in the infamous Stalag Luft III as PoW number 3132 Acting Flight Lieutenant 106673 J.D. Hill RAF. The actor Donald Pleasance claimed that James Hill was the inspiration for the forger in the 1963 film *The Great Escape*.

After the war he made several films for Rank's Children's Film Foundation, as well as documentaries. His many credits in television include *The Avengers*, *The Saint* (he wrote and directed many episodes), *Black Beauty* and *The Bellstone Fox* series. Perhaps he will be best remembered as the director of *Born Free*.

James Douglas Hill DFC died in London on 8 October 1994 aged seventy-five.

Joseph Hobson-Jagger

The Man Who Broke the Bank at Monte Carlo

In the little-visited graveyard of Bethel Independent Methodist Church at Shelf, Bradford, are the mortal remains of the 'Man Who Broke the Bank at Monte Carlo'.

Joseph Hobson-Jagger was born at Cockhill, near Shelf, in September 1830. He was an engineer by trade, being employed at Henry Bottomley's Clough Mills, Shelf. There he was deemed an expert on spindles and noted for his intelligence and jovial personality. But it was his knowledge of the French spindles used in roulette wheels, rather than spindles used in the woollen industry, that he put to a profitable use.

In 1875 while on holiday in Monte Carlo his interest was kindled by the roulette cylinders in the casino, so much so that he employed a team of clerks for a week to note

the numbers appearing at every table. It became apparent that one cylinder showed a tendency to throw a higher percentage of certain numbers. Though he was not a gambler (he was a Methodist lay preacher) he knew he was on to something. He struck his first bet on 17 July 1875, and went on to win 2 million francs in eight days.

Crowds of holidaymakers made a bee-line for the casino as news spread that something unusual was happening. The 'Lucky Englishman' continued to pile up his winnings until the casino operators switched the cylinders among the tables. But Jagger had secretly marked the crucial cylinder, and in the end the casino had to close temporarily while better quality cylinders were substituted. His winnings were the largest made at Monte Carlo to that time, and would be equivalent to around £2m today. According to the popular jargon he had broken the bank necessitating the fetching of more gold coins in boxes from the head office.

He returned to England immediately, indeed he had to, for in those days the casino authorities went to great lengths to persuade winning gamblers back to the tables. In fact he never left England again. He settled with his wife Matilda, it is thought in Spicer Street, Little Horton, and bought a great deal of property in the Roundhill Street district.

His great wealth did not, alas, bring him happiness; he made the mistake of retiring to a life of luxury! This proved unwise, for a life of idleness did not suit his intellectual ability, and he became subject to long bouts of acute depression and lethargy.

He died on 25 April 1892 at the age of sixty-one, reputedly 'tired of life'.

David Hockney CH

Artist

From comparatively humble beginnings, David Hockney has become one of the most popular artists of his generation.

Born on 9 July 1937, he was the fourth of five children, the family residing at Hutton Terrace, Eccleshill. In 1948 David was awarded a scholarship to Bradford Grammar School. While there he decided that he wanted to be an artist and his cartoons were a regular feature of the school magazine. Aged fourteen, he asked to join the junior art school affiliated to the Bradford School of Art. His request was refused and he remained at Bradford Grammar until he was sixteen. He then attended the Bradford School of Art.

During his early days he would work at his drawings for 10–12 hours a day. His draughtsmanship marked him out as exceptional. Later he attended the Royal College of Art in London, then went on to lecture at Maidstone College of Art and the universities of Iowa, Colorado, California, Los Angeles and Berkeley. Many one-man shows in the US and Europe followed, as did biographical publications, including *David Hockney* by David Hockney.

David has drawn and painted an astonishing range of subjects. He is also an outstanding stage designer and has experimented with photography and new technologies. His overwhelming talent is as a draughtsman and he has long crusaded for drawing not to be overlooked by art colleges. His paintings of Californian subjects vibrate with colour. His portraits, frequently moving, are of his mother, his friends and his dachshunds. His work is widely accessible and much loved by the general public.

David's work is featured in countless museums and galleries around the world including the Tate in London, the National Gallery of Australia and the Museum of Modern Art in New York. Despite worldwide fame, he has never shed his Bradford roots. As a friend of the late Jonathan Silver, he has used Salt's Mill as his gallery. He has been a generous benefactor to his old school and given his name to the Hockney Theatre.

He was once quoted as saying 'Everybody should be allowed to escape'. His own escape from the confines of a Bradford childhood has taken him all over the world. In 1997, the year of David Hockney's sixtieth birthday, he was made a Companion of Honour in the Queen's Birthday Honours List.

Sir Fred Hoyle

Astronomer

'A genius is someone who has two good ideas', said the broadcaster and mathematician Jacob Bronowski. By that definition Fred Hoyle qualifies with ease.

Born in Primrose Lane, Gilstead, Bingley, on 24 June 1915, he was educated at the infant and primary schools in Eldwick, and sang in the choir at St Wilfrid's Church in Gilstead, achieving many awards with the church's Band of Hope temperance group. He then went on to Bingley Grammar School where he established himself as a mathematical prodigy. As a young boy he was always interested in astronomy and after his father bought him his first telescope he would sit on the front step night after night under freezing cloudless skies, gazing at the stars. At Bingley Grammar School his talent won him a place at Emmanuel College, Cambridge.

In 1939 he became a fellow of St John's College Cambridge, and during the Second World War he conducted scientific research for the Admiralty with the rank of commodore, visiting German radar installations in 1945.

After the war he returned to his first love, astronomy, and became famous for opposing the 'Big Bang' theory of the origin of the universe. By 1957 he was a Fellow of the Royal Society and he was knighted in 1972. He also served as President of the Royal Astronomical Society from 1971 to 1973. He collected many awards, among them the Crafoord Prize from the Royal Swedish Academy of Sciences. He also penned such classics as *A for Andromeda* (1962), which was turned into a TV series, and was a much-acclaimed author of science fiction and popular science books.

In his early years, Hoyle was certainly brash, challenging his colleagues with a bluntness they were not used to. He believed that if he fired off enough ideas some would at least hit the target. He did not think he would be right every time, but others did – and he was heavily criticised when he was wrong.

In later life he moved to Bournemouth but would still make the odd visit to his beloved Eldwick, and was keen to walk up to Dick Hudson's to see if any of his old friends still lived in the village. He also still followed Bradford City, the team he had supported with his father as a child. Hoyle's father had also taken him to watch the cricket at Wagon Lane in Bingley. In 1975 he was awarded an honorary degree from Bradford University.

Sir Fred Hoyle died in Bournemouth's Christchurch Hospital in August 2001 aged eighty-six.

Private Matthew Hughes VC

Victoria Cross Recipient in the Crimea

On 26 June 1857 at a ceremony in Hyde Park, Queen Victoria presented soldiers and sailors with the Victoria Cross. This was the first presentation of the newly instituted award, and among those who received it was Private Matthew Hughes from Bradford.

Matthew Hughes was born in Bradford in March 1822, son of Samuel and Alice Hughes. In March 1840 he enlisted in the 7th Royal Fusiliers at Leeds at eighteen and was given the regimental number 1496. He was discharged at his own request in January 1844 on payment of £20 but re-enlisted five months later in June and was given a new regimental number, 1879. He was both promoted and demoted over the next few years, in some cases being a sergeant then reduced to the rank of private, and he also committed the odd custodial offence, making quite a colourful career.

On 28 March 1854 Britain and France declared war on Russia after her invasion of Turkish provinces. Britain prepared to send an expeditionary force to the Crimea, and among the troops were Hughes's 7th Royal Fusiliers.

In a war where more casualties were caused by the climate and disease, some of the hardest fought battles were during the siege of Sevastopol, especially in the so-called 'Quarries'. It was here for acts of bravery between 7 and 18 June 1855 that Private Hughes earned the Victoria Cross.

The citation in the *London Gazette* of 24 February 1857 reads: 'Private Matthew Hughes, 7th Royal Fusiliers was noticed by Colonel Campbell 90th Light Infantry on the 7th June, 1855, at the storming of the Quarries, twice going for ammunition under heavy fire, across open ground; and being wounded by a shell in the knee, he also went to the front and brought in Pte John Hampton, who was lying severely wounded; and on the 18th of June, 1855, he volunteered to bring in Lieutenant Hobson, 7th Royal fusiliers, who was lying severely wounded, and in the act of doing so was severely wounded himself (by a musket ball in the foot).'

Private Hampton, whose life Hughes saved, survived the war and was admitted to his pension in 1856. He was still living in Carlisle in 1875. After serving over two years in the Crimea, three years in the East Indies and a posting in Gibraltar, Hughes was discharged at the depot at Walmer in Kent on 18 September 1861. He was then forty-three and he was described as 5ft 7in tall with brown hair and grey eyes. His intended occupation was labourer and his place of residence was to be Bradford.

He was married to Helen and lived at 147 Wapping Road, Bradford, where she was lodging as a housekeeper and he was the beerhouse keeper. He died at this address on 9 January 1882 aged sixty and is buried in section N388 at Undercliffe Cemetery. Records show that Helen continued to run the beerhouse after his death. He was lying forgotten in a pauper's grave until recently when a new headstone recording Hughes's VC was unveiled.

David Jeffries

Isle of Man TT Champion

The name Jeffries has been synonymous with Shipley and the world of motorcycling for nearly a century, but David, who died in 2003 in a high-speed crash, took that reputation to new heights.

David Jeffries was born on 18 September 1972 in Baildon. He attended Hoyle Court First School and Ladderbanks, both in Baildon, then Salt's Grammar School in Saltaire.

Leaving school at sixteen he became an apprentice plant engineer at Brown's of Otley until he was made redundant at the age of twenty, but this was no problem. Being mechanically minded, he worked on any engine with wheels, and even spent some time as an HGV driver. David was making his own way and had not become involved in the well-known family business, Allan Jeffries of Shipley.

David's great-grandfather, Jo Jeffries, a pioneer motorist who had covered more than 100,000 miles by the end of the First World War, had started the business. Jo's son Allan was the first member of the family to enter the world of motorcycle sport, competing in the TT Championships. He was works rider for the Scott motorcycle factory at Saltaire for whom he competed in all aspects of the sport, including trials, scrambling, road racing and speedway. He switched to become works rider for Triumph, where the Jeffries name became nationally known as he won every major event in the country. He retired in 1949 and his sons Tony and Nick were left to carry the banner for the family.

David's father Tony competed in road racing from 1968, establishing himself on the international circuit and winning a number of TT races, but five years later he was left paralysed after a racing accident at the Mallory Park circuit in Leicestershire. He went on to run the BMW motorcycle dealership in Shipley. Nick Jeffries, David's uncle, also established himself as a specialist in road racing, winning top races at the TT as recently as 1993.

But it was David who took the highest honours. He began riding bikes when he was four, taking part in his first senior road race in 1990, aged eighteen. His first taste of TT was in 1996, where he took the best newcomer's award, but missed 1997 after breaking his collar-bone riding a road bike. He went on to win titles and break records all over the world, culminating in 2002 when he became the only rider in the history of TT races to win the top three titles in three consecutive championships. Known as DJ by his fans, the powerfully built 14 stone, 6ft 2in figure was highly respected for his skill and determination, and as an ambassador for motorcycling.

The thirty-year-old racer had become a hero for his exploits, which included lifting a TT title for the ninth time in 2000, as well as setting a new lap record averaging more than 127mph along the Isle of Man's 37 miles of twisting roads. He had already earned a place among the Manx TT greats and was among the favourites in 2003, hoping to break the 200mph barrier on parts of the circuit.

On 29 May 2003, David had just completed a 125mph practice lap when his Suzuki motorcycle crashed when it was travelling at an estimated 160mph. David was killed. He was one of the best bikers of his generation. The respect accorded to David by motorcycling fans was typified by the huge number of tributes that poured in from around the world. Shipley and Saltaire came to a standstill on the day of his funeral at Nab Wood Cemetery.

Joe Johnson

World Snooker Champion

Joe Johnson's win in the 1986 World Snooker Championship was the biggest shock the event had ever witnessed. Make no mistake, he was a very good player, but his achievements had never quite matched his talent – until then.

Born in Bradford on 29 July 1952, it was as a young teenager that Joe developed a flair for snooker, taking part in amateur tournaments in between employment as a trainee mechanic and a pipe layer. He was for many years the holder of the highest break recorded by an amateur – 140 in Middlesbrough in 1978 – and he was also the runner-up in the 1978 World Amateur Championship final in Sydney. This prompted him to turn professional in 1979.

Joe, ranked world no. 16 when the 1986 World Championship began, was quoted at 150–1 for the title, not unduly generous odds given that he had failed to win a tournament in his seven years as a professional. A 16–8 victory over Tony Knowles put him in the final but Steve Davis, attempting to exorcise the ghost of the previous year, had barely been tested in coming through the other half and was again expecting to win. From 8–8 at the end of the first day, Johnson claimed a 13–11 lead going into the final session. Still many believed Davis would turn it round, but no comeback was forthcoming and Johnson seemed to play without nerves in clinching an 18–12 victory. With his two-tone patterned shoes and twitching eyebrows that were to become famous, he remains the Crucible's most unlikely winner.

A down-to-earth Yorkshireman, Joe celebrated with his mates back at the Snooker Centre in Bradford. The following season, he endured a nightmare tour, but bounced back to form in the World Championship. Against all the odds he reached the final again. This time, though, there was to be no fairytale final and he was beaten 18–14 by – guess who? Steve Davis, of course.

His other career highlights were winning the Scottish Masters (1987) and Norwich Union Grand Prix (1989). His future may be on the embryonic seniors' tour, but no one can take away those wonderful memories of May 1986 when he had the world of snooker at his feet.

Benjamin and William Jowett
Car Manufacturing Pioneers

Benjamin and William Jowett set up a two-man general engineering business in 1901 but were to become thriving motor manufacturers in less than twenty years. All this took place well away from the Midlands, which was then the centre of the British car manufacturing industry.

Benjamin (born 1877) and William (born 1880) were the two sons of Jane and Wilfrid Jowett of 87 Kensington Street, Girlington. They were educated at Fairweather Green School in the afternoons, spending the mornings from 6.30a.m. working in the local mill. In their early teens they started working at their father's blacksmith's shop and soon became conversant with everything mechanical from bicycles to steam engines and boilers.

In 1901, with their sister Ruth, they formed the Jowett Motor Manufacturing Company, working from Church Street, Manningham. The business moved to Back Burlington Street and then in 1907 they bought premises in Grosvenor Road, Manningham. Their first prototype car was developed in 1906 and production started in 1910. Although only forty-eight cars were produced before the First World War, ninety men were employed on car production and general engineering before the factory was turned over to the manufacture of munitions for the war effort.

After the war Jowett Cars Ltd was registered with a capital of £30,000 and car production began in earnest at their new premises at Idle. Production peaked in 1927 at 3,474 vehicles. The hallmark of Jowett's success was the horizontally opposed twin-cylinder engine which had first been developed in 1906 with a capacity of 815cc, and had been enlarged through the years to 1,005cc for the Bradford van in 1946. By the time production ceased in 1953 it had become the engine with the longest production run ever – forty-three years.

Benjamin was the designer and William concentrated on the engineering aspect, spending much of his time in the works. In 1935 Jowett Cars Ltd became a public company and Benjamin resigned. This was a difficult time for the company because Jowetts were competing with the mass production of larger companies. Up until this point they had never borrowed to finance expansion.

Small losses were recorded in the late 1930s, outside directors were brought in, and William eventually retired in 1939. Both brothers retained financial control until after the Second World War when they sold out to Charles Clore of City & Central Investments Ltd. William went on to develop and expand Bristol Tractors Ltd of Earby and both brothers had a financial interest in many local businesses.

The simple twin-cylinder Bradford van was the backbone of postwar production, with over 40,000 made between 1946 and 1953. The Javelin was introduced in 1948 with a 1,500cc flat-four engine. Its radical design involved huge capital investment. The bodies were supplied by Briggs Brothers of Doncaster at a predetermined rate and the supply of these soon exceeded sales of the cars, which

Benjamin Jowett.   William Jowett.

had been slow because of gearbox problems and was due more importantly to the fact that it was an expensive car at an austere time. The Jupiter sports model was introduced in 1950 and won its class at the Le Mans 24-Hour Race three years in succession, but with fewer than 1,000 manufactured it never made a significant contribution to company profits.

It was decided to wind up the company in 1953; the premises were sold to International Harvesters in 1954. (The Enterprise Five complex now stands on the site.)

William died in 1955 aged seventy-four and Benjamin in 1963 aged eighty-six, leaving behind the legacy of a unique car of distinctive design.

Les Kellett

International Professional Wrestler

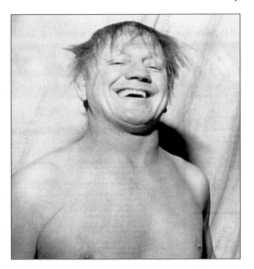

In the 1960s Les Kellett's name was synonymous with the world of professional wrestling, introduced to the nation by Kent Walton via Saturday afternoon television.

Les Kellett was born at Laisterdyke in 1916, the son of Bill Kellett, an engineer well known in that area, and Sarah. He left Bradford Moor School at the age of fourteen and followed his father into engineering. He learned amateur wrestling at a young age but did not pursue it. However, he did play rugby league for Bradford Northern Juniors and Yorkshire.

During the Second World War he saw service in the Merchant Navy as an engineer. After 1945 Les went back to amateur wrestling and was taught by Joe Hill, who had a small gym in Swain House Road where a little shed at the back accommodated his students. By the 1950s he was earning between £40 and £50 a match and averaging five or six matches a week spread all over the country – quite an amazing income. He could be wrestling in Leeds, and in a few hours have to travel up to Edinburgh, Aberdeen or down to Cardiff. He used to say 'I can't understand how anyone could fight so many times a week and absorb all that punishment'. But he did.

Les's daft-as-brush act earned him the nickname 'The Clown Prince of Europe', but this clown became the professional Light Heavyweight Champion of Britain. TV appearances and matches at venues all over the north, including Bradford's St George's Hall, made him a household name. He was nominated for Sports Personality of the Year in the 1960s. He taught both Jimmy Saville and Harvey Smith to wrestle.

He retired in about 1975, and for many years he and his wife Margaret lived in an old black-and-white house in Thornton Road. The building contained a café called the Terminus which Margaret ran. Behind the café on two acres of land Les sometimes bred pigs, and at one time he had 50 head of cattle.

He said that although he made a lot of money during thirty-five years in the ring, wrestling Monday to Saturday, it had not made him a rich man. Indeed, to supplement his income he sometimes cleaned cars at Stroud Drummond Riley's woollen mill in Lumb Lane, a job he enjoyed, especially when he was required to chauffeur the company's clients from the station and airport. It was a far cry from the dizzy heights he reached as a wrestling star.

After moving to a nursing home in Ilkley, Les Kellett died peacefully in his sleep January 2002 aged eighty-six.

Ken Kitson

Actor, Director, Writer and Poet

Ken Kitson was born on 7 July 1946 at Seal Street but his family later moved to Brackenholme Road, Buttershaw, where he attended St Michael's and All Angels' Primary School in Shelf, and later Wibsey Secondary High School.

Leaving school at fifteen, he went to English Electric as apprentice machine fitter, but didn't like the job and decided that he wanted to move into printing. He obtained a list of all the printers in Bradford and on his fifty-fourth cold call he was accepted at Wheeldon's Printers near the Towers Hall in Manchester Road. After finishing his apprenticeship he was employed by Midget Press, Great Horton, as a manager.

With a flair for acting he joined a Theatre Group at Wilsden called The Barnstormers with his friend John Duttine. His job as a printer was now becoming a secondary interest to acting, and when the call came from John Duttine in London asking Kitson to join him and two other budding actors to share a flat, it was too good an opportunity to miss.

Now aged twenty-three he earned a place at London's East 15 drama school run by Maggie Bury (originally from Queensbury). After three years he had developed an all-round acting ability and secured a diploma in fencing and stage fighting. He has used this over many years to choreograph fights and fencing sequences on stage and in films.

It was John Slater of *Z Cars* who helped him sign up with his first agent after seeing him in a small part in *A Midsummer Night's Dream*. One of his first parts was with Norman Wisdom in *Nobody is Norman* and another with Pebble Mill's Second City First productions, where one of his early leads was in the production of *A Wish for Wally's Mother*. He played a retarded character with Ruth Dunning as his mother, and won national acclaim.

Since those early days he has now amassed over 250 stage, TV and film credits including *Coronation Street*, *Get Some In*, *Van Der Valk*, *Danger UXB*, *Chance in a Million*, *All Creatures Great and Small*, *Ripping Yarns*, *Minder*, *The Professionals*, *Ruth Rendell Mysteries*, *Heartbeat*, *Emmerdale*, *The Bill*, *London's Burning* and *Dalziel and Pascoe*.

Perhaps one of his most endearing roles is in *The Last of the Summer Wine* where he portrays the local constable, a part he has played in between other commitments for many years. He was recently awarded an engraved glass bowl for his contribution to this series. He is currently writing and directing a play, to be filmed in the near future, called *Fistful of Dreams*. This gentle comedy set in the eccentric world of Britain's cowboy clubs has a host of top stars.

Francis Laidler

Theatre Entrepreneur

Yorkshire theatre magnate Francis Laidler was one of the best-known personalities connected with the British stage; his pantomimes were legendary.

He was born at Thornaby-on-Tees on 7 January 1867, the son of a surgeon. After a few years in service at the National Provincial Bank in Stokesley, he moved to Bradford in 1888 at the age of twenty-one as secretary to Hammond's (Bradford) Brewery Co. Ltd, Manchester Road. In 1902 he became a partner leaseholder with Mr W.J. Piper of the Prince's Theatre, Bradford. On Mr Piper's death he took full control, at the same time relinquishing his connection with Hammond's.

After taking over the Theatre Royal, Leeds, some years later, he was responsible for many successful touring operations. He acquired a controlling interest in many northern theatres. It was through his influence that the Bradford Alhambra was built in 1914, and this was the scene of many of his greatest successes. He was always more keen on staging variety, reviews, musicals and pantomimes than straight plays. His first Bradford pantomimes were staged at the Princess Theatre, with such stars as Hetty King, Vesta Tilley and others. It is estimated that over his lifetime he produced more than 250 pantomimes. His production of *Humpty Dumpty* at the Theatre Royal, Leeds, in 1945 ran for 22 weeks, at that time the longest run of any pantomime in England.

Mr Laidler always donated to charitable organisations, such as the Bradford Cinderella Club, the Royal National Lifeboat Institution (of which he was made an honorary life governor) and the *Yorkshire Evening Post* Boots for Bairns Fund. Mr Laidler also served on Bradford Council as Conservative Councillor for West Ward from 1907 to 1910.

Perhaps Francis Laidler is best remembered by Bradfordians for his 'Sunbeams'. This chorus of little girls was initially recruited from local schoolchildren and their welfare was always paramount to him. Months prior to the opening of a pantomime, mothers and their young girls would be seen queuing down Morley Street, hoping for selection. The chosen few would stay in comfortable hostel accommodation and receive education from qualified teachers throughout the pantomime season.

During his later life Laidler occupied a suite in Bradford's Victoria Hotel, sharing it for some thirty years with his second wife Gladys. It was she who took over his empire when he died on 6 January 1955 in the Duke of York Home, Bradford, aged eighty-eight. He was described as 'a man of high principles, who soon made it clear to numerous artists that he would not tolerate anything risqué, or blue, on his stages'.

Jim Laker

Surrey and England Cricketer

Who was the greatest cricketer the Bradford League has ever produced? There is only one possible answer – Jim Laker

The brilliant off-spinner for Surrey and England was born in 1922 at 36 Norwood Road, Frizinghall, and attended Salt's Boys' High School. He spent his school holidays playing with his pals on Northcliffe Fields in Shipley. Laker first played for Saltaire Cricket Club as a sixteen-year-old, having been invited to join the club by Mr Alf Burgoyne, who served as secretary at Roberts Park. In those days, however, Laker had not cultivated the off-spin that was to make him world famous.

Like any Yorkshire boy with a love of cricket, Laker nursed ambitions to play for his county, but was rejected after an invitation to perform in the nets. He was bitterly disappointed, but was always big enough and honest enough to admit that at the time he was simply not good enough. It was written many times during his career that Yorkshire let him slip through their fingers, but it was never true, they just did not think he was good enough to play for them and, at the time they made their decision, he said they were right.

Having developed his successful off-spin he was a completely different type of player when Surrey were given permission by Yorkshire to sign him on special registration in 1946. Yorkshire did make a late approach to Laker to see if he would return, but by then his loyalties were quite rightly with Surrey.

He reserved one of his greatest-ever achievements for home soil. It was the Test Trial at Park Avenue in 1950 where he bowled for England against The Rest and took 8 wickets for 2 runs in 14 overs, arguably the best bowling return ever. Laker went on to help Surrey win the County Championship in seven successive seasons from 1952–58. However, 'Laker's Match' will always remain the Test against Australia at Old Trafford in 1956 when he took 19 of the 20 wickets for just 90 runs. In 1962 having come out of retirement he played 30 matches for Essex before finally calling it a day in 1964.

Throughout his first-class career he took 1,944 wickets at an average of 18.4 runs apiece, and held 270 catches. On eleven occasions he exceeded 100 wickets in a season, his best summer being in 1950 when he took 166 wickets at 15.32 runs apiece. His England career of 46 matches spanned 1947 to 1959, and in all Tests he took 193 wickets at an average of 21.24.

Jim Laker went on to a successful career as a journalist and commentator on both radio and television alongside great men such as John Arlott and Richie Benaud. He died in 1986 aged sixty-four.

Dougie Lampkin MBE
World Champion Motorcycle Trials Rider

Silsden: while the valley bottom carries traffic, the moors carry dreams. They inspire ramblers and artists, as the eye leaps from crag to boulder and beck to pasture. Landscapes like this have made the Lampkins.

Dougie was born on 23 March 1976. The family lived at Addingham Moorhead, overlooking Silsden. His father Martin was then the reigning world champion motorcycle trials rider and had already bought a 50cc mini-bike in case Dougie was interested. He was, and could ride it by the time he was three. Aged nine he entered his first event at Pateley Bridge – and being a Lampkin, he won.

Dougie attended Addingham Primary School and later St Cuthbert's in Pateley Bridge, where the family had moved to run the local pub, the Miners Arms. Into his teens he was still winning events. On leaving school at fifteen he knew he had the makings of a great trials rider, so to help finance his chosen career he became a navvy on the Knaresborough bypass, picked up at 6.15a.m. and dropped off at 7.45p.m. after a twelve-hour day shift.

That was in 1992; in 1993 he became the youngest European Champion at the age of seventeen getting two firsts, and two second places in the six events. From 1994 to 1996 he was in the top positions of the British and World Championships. Since then he has won a remarkable six consecutive World Outdoor and Indoor championships, an unparalleled and unbroken run which shows no sign of ending.

He is determined to break Jordi Tarres's record of seven world titles (in nine years, not consecutive), a record which, when achieved, will be no more than he deserves. He was awarded the MBE in the 2002 New Year Honours List, a tribute to the sport and a fine young man following in the Lampkin family tradition.

Wilfrid Lawson

Actor

A character both off stage and on, Wilfrid Lawson was born in 1901 in Harris Street, off Barkerend Road, Bradford. He was the son of John Mitchell Worsnop who was an artist-photographer and is believed to have once employed the notorious murderer Charles Peace to make picture frames. He was also the official photographer at the opening of the Bradford Technical College in May 1882.

Wilfrid became a pupil at Hanson School and although he never appeared in any of the school plays, he played in the school orchestra. It was his half-brother who was connected with the stage, and during school holidays Wilfrid would help him with the occasional acting part. After attending Hanson he went to Bradford Technical College to study chemistry and dyeing with the intention of entering the textile trade. Then Alfred Denville's company visited the Bradford Theatre Royal with *Joseph and his Brethren*. The company needed extras and Wilfrid applied. He was so good that Denville kept him on and later advertised him as 'his youngest leading man', for although he was a hefty lad, he was still in his teens.

Wildfrid eventually left Denville to join Ernest E. Norris, an actor-manager who used to come to Bradford's Theatre Royal for summer repertory seasons, and toured with him. He appeared with the Norris company at the Theatre Royal in 1917 and a little afterwards, having reached military age, he joined the Royal Flying Corps. On demobilisation he returned to the stage by way of repertory and in eight years played over 400 parts.

Once he was appearing at the Elephant and Castle in *Sweeney Todd* and was seen by George Bernard Shaw, who suggested he joined the Shaw Company. His last appearance in Bradford was at the Alhambra in 1931 with this company.

After many successful plays, and even one pantomime appearance at the Lyric Theatre, Hammersmith, he was well established in the capital's theatrical world. He then went to the USA to appear in a play on Broadway and from there went to Hollywood under contract with the Fox Film Company. At the outbreak of the Second World War he was in Hollywood but became the first actor to fly home from there to offer his services to his country.

In later life he played admirable character parts in such films as *Room at the Top* and *The Wrong Box*. He even had a cameo part in *The Likely Lads* as Terry's grandfather.

Wilfrid Lawson, the Bradford-born stage, film and television actor, died at his home in Holland Park, London, in 1966, aged sixty-five years.

George Layton
Actor, Writer and Producer

In a testimonial presented to George Layton, John Fernald, Director of the Royal Academy of Dramatic Art (RADA), wrote, 'Your talent is such that you have profited to the full by your academy experience, and I could hardly be more pleased than I am by the work you have done. Good luck to you in your professional career, in which I am quite sure success will be yours.' Indeed it is!

Born on 2 March 1942 at St Luke's Hospital, George Layton was the son of Austrian parents who settled in Bradford and lived at 48 Bertram Road, Manningham. He attended Lilycroft Primary School, where one of his teachers, Mrs Hartney, set George on the way to a career on stage by encouraging him in prominent parts in school plays.

George's next school, Belle Vue Grammar, needed some persuasion that he was made for an acting career. While he was a pupil there during the 1950s he was involved in his own extra-mural activities at the Bradford Civic Playhouse, where the secretary received a written request from George's headmaster asking that he be discouraged from participating in the theatre. Fortunately, the secretary had recognised George's thespian talent and potential, and she went to the school personally to persuade the headmaster to withdraw his request.

After school in Bradford, George worked for a while at the Royal Infirmary. He then gained a scholarship to RADA, where he won the Emile Littler Award for the Most Promising Actor. His professional stage career was launched, enabling him to do what he always wanted to do and loved.

George has played leading parts in the West End, on Broadway and in Australia. Recent appearances include Fagin in Cameron Mackintosh's production of *Oliver* at the London Palladium, Amos Hart (Mr Cellophane) in *Chicago* at the Adelphi Theatre, Bert Challenor in the nationally acclaimed production of *Comedians* at the Oxford Stage company, and the lead in a new American play called *Of Blessed Memory* at the King's Head Theatre, Islington.

He has combined his acting with a successful writing career. On television he starred in and wrote for *Doctor in the House*, in which he played the role of Dr Paul Collier. Bombardier Solomons in *It Ain't Half Hot Mum*, and Des the car mechanic in *Minder* were two of George's other creations. He was also one of the three presenters in the first series of *That's Life*. He wrote the last two series and the Christmas special of *Robin's Nest*, occasionally appearing as the amoral Vernon Potter.

He created and wrote two award-winning series for television, *Don't Wait Up* (six seasons), starring Nigel Havers and Tony Britton, and *Executive Stress* (three seasons) starring Penelope Keith. Both these shows were aired throughout the world. George has recently completed a twenty-part series on television programmes in the 1970s, which he wrote and narrated, to be seen on ITV at a future date.

His best-selling book *The Fib* (Macmillan) has sold over a quarter of a million copies and is on the National Curriculum. His second book, *The Swap* (Macmillan),

has also been published in America and was chosen by the New York Public Library for their *Top 100 Annual List*. George regularly presents his one-man show in the theatre reading from both his books. Both *The Fib* and *The Swap* are based on his growing up in Bradford in the 1950s. He has recently completed a screenplay based on *The Swap*, which he will direct (in Bradford and surrounding districts).

George's voice will be familiar to many children for the animated cartoon series he has narrated for television – *Pigeon Street, Joshua Jones, Dig and Dug* – and many audio-books. He has also done numerous voice-overs for television commercials, especially that cult hero from the Tetley teafolk, the gormless Sydney. Recent television roles have been the hapless Alan Brookes in the BBC comedy-drama *Sunburn* and Dr Maurice Jacobson in *Metropolis* for Granada TV. He recently appeared as Jerzy in the critically acclaimed production of *More Lies about Jerzy* at the New End Theatre, London.

In 1999 he was surprised with 'the big red book' by Michael Aspel on *This is Your Life* and in July 2000 he received an honorary doctorate from the University of Bradford in recognition of his work as an actor and writer.

David Lee
Pantomime Producer

David Lee, Managing Director of Pantoni Pantomimes, has produced over 200 pantomimes in all parts of the UK over the past twenty-five years. He is a remarkable producer with more than a hint of the success enjoyed by his predecessor Francis Laidler.

David was born Arthur Walter Backhouse at St Luke's Hospital, Bradford, on 15 September 1949. The first three years of his life were spent at the family home in Haigh Row, Undercliffe, and in 1952 the family moved to 10 Manor Street, Eccleshill, where he lived until 1979.

He was not from a showbusiness family. His father Omar worked for the Bradford building company J. & J. Obank, and his mother and maternal grandmother worked in several woollen mills, including the one which stood on the site of what is now Bradford's Industrial Museum.

David's first introduction to show-business was when his mother and grandmother took him to see a Sunday school pantomime production of *Dick Whittington* in Laisterdyke in 1951. Being a very active child nothing much kept him occupied for very long, but he was captivated by the show. So enthralled was he that his grandmother suggested taking him to the Alhambra to see one of the wonderful Francis Laidler pantomime productions. That experience was to make an enormous impression on the boy.

Regular visits to the Bradford Alhambra pantomimes fuelled David's enthusiasm and in 1961, on the advice of his Wellington Road Primary School headmaster Mr Proctor, his mother started taking him to the Gainsborough Stage School situated in Albion Court, Kirkgate. Here he discovered the songs of Al Jolson and started performing them in stage school productions and for family gatherings. It was during this time that he adopted the surname Lee, from the Jolson song 'Waiting for the Robert E. Lee'.

In 1962 he joined the Happy Times Concert Party headed by Margaret Wood, wife of the Bradford photographer C.H. Wood OBE (famous for his aerial photographs of the region which appeared in the *Telegraph & Argus*). He gained valuable performance experience appearing in hundreds of shows around the West

Riding of Yorkshire. He also studied the theory of music, and learned the ukulele and banjo from Bradford entertainer Tony Weldon.

In 1965 he left Hutton School in Eccleshill to appear in his first summer season at the Floral Hall in Whitby for the Keighley-based radio and television organist Freda Hall, billed as 'The Queen of the Keys'. Shortly after the summer David's voice broke, so, he said, 'I had to get a proper job!' He was accepted by the department store Brown Muff & Co. Ltd, joining their radio and television department in Howard House on Broadway. He was noted for his people skills and dedication by his buyer, Mr Bromby, and by the store's chairman, Ernest Marriott MBE. He was sent to Bradford Technical College to study retail distribution. It was in 1968, by which time his voice was settled and he was regularly appearing in working men's clubs in the region, that David was honoured to be asked to take over for Al Jolson Junior (when the entertainer had to return unexpectedly to the United States) at the Ritz (then a casino) in Brighouse and the Savoy Club in Wakefield. By 1970 he was earning the equivalent of his Brown Muff weekly salary in one night, and had to make the decision: to re-enter show business or stay at the store. Show business won.

His second summer season was at Morecambe Bay Holiday Camp, followed by his first pantomime in Southport. Numerous seasons and tours followed. In May 1977 he appeared at the Bradford Alhambra in *The New Minstrel Show* as Al Jolson. In 1978 David moved into the production field, predominantly as a pantomime producer presenting his first pantomime *Goldilocks and the Three Bears*, starring Liverpool comedian Johnny Hackett. The following year he presented Valentine Dyall and Brian Marshall in *Aladdin*, and Charlie Drake and Tammy Jones in *Jack and the Beanstalk*.

Over the years David has employed many of the top names in show business, including Australian singing star Natalie Imbruglia, Billy Pearce, Wayne Sleep, Alvin Stardust, Jeremy Beadle, Shane Ritchie, Jack Douglas, Craig Douglas, Susan Maughan, Roy Castle, John Pertwee and Ted Rogers, as well as showbiz legends Tommy Trinder and Sandy Powell. David has also presented several small jazz concerts starring George Melly and Humphrey Lyttelton.

David Lee is also a songwriter, having written over a hundred songs, mainly for pantomime. In 1981 he moved to Maidstone and at present lives at St Leonard's-on-Sea with his business partner, West End and international choreographer and production director Rita Proctor. In 1994 he was honoured by being elected to the most prestigious show business fraternity, the Grand Order of Water Rats.

Samuel Cunliffe Lister

Wool Baron

In the early nineteenth century the people of Bradford could never have imagined that the time would come when on the site of the first Manningham mill there would one day be a motive power at work equal to three times the then total horsepower of all the factories in the town, and that in place of one small mill that existed there, there would be an establishment covering nearly 11 acres of ground: Manningham Mills.

Samuel Cunliffe Lister was born on 1 January 1815 at Calverley Old Hall, the fourth son of Ellis Cunliffe Lister who, in 1832, became one of Bradford's two Members of Parliament under the Reform Act.

Samuel's early years were spent at a private school at Clapham Common in London, where he completed his education. On leaving school he went to Liverpool and was employed in a counting house, where he remained for a short time, ultimately settling down in Bradford in the woollen industry. In 1837 his father built a worsted mill in Bradford for him and his brother John. Their partnership flourished until 1845 when John retired.

An inventor of sorts, Samuel had over 150 patents to his name. His first, in 1841, was a swivel shuttle for inserting a silk figure on to a plain background. This was followed three years later by one for fringing shawls. A wool-combing machine he bought from George Edmund Donnisthorpe proved unsatisfactory, so Lister worked on it for three years until he had produced a machine capable of handling wool in the way he wanted. Various improvements followed and there was soon a demand for the machine, which was built for £200 and sold for £1,200. His machine made the vast trade based on Australian wool possible.

There were dangers in his inventive obsessions. In 1855 he first thought of using silk waste, and spent a number of years and vast sums of money trying to evolve a machine capable of doing the task he wanted. By 1864 he succeeded after spending over £¼ million on the project, but other spinners would not look at the machine and he faced ruin. People then suddenly became interested; and silk waste from China, India and Italy, bought at 6d per pound, was converted into silk velvets, carpets, imitation sealskins and poplins. After years at the apex of the world's wool combing industry, he amassed a second fortune, and when the original Manningham Mills were destroyed by fire, he rebuilt them on an even larger scale.

He was reputed to have paid £1 million for his estates at Swinton Park, Jervaulx and Middleham. Although a hard businessman, he was most generous to Bradford, and in 1870 he sold his home, Manningham Hall, with its estate, to Bradford Corporation at less than half its value, and contributed £47,000 towards the Cartwright Memorial Hall. Bradford thus acquired, in perpetuity, an open space that was named Lister Park in his honour.

Lister was a Justice of the Peace in both the North and West Ridings, and in 1887 he became High Sheriff of Yorkshire. The Society of Arts awarded him the

Albert Medal in 1886 and five years later he was created the first Baron Masham. He received an honorary doctorate from Leeds University, and in 1898 was made a Freeman of Bradford. A statue of Lister was unveiled at the main entrance to Lister Park on 15 May 1875 by the Rt Hon W.E. Forster, MP for Bradford.

Samuel Lister's long and active life came to an end when he was ninety-one, on 2 February 1906, at his home in Swinton Park, Masham. The funeral took place on 7 February at Addingham Parish Church.

Yvonne McGregor MBE

Olympic Bronze Medallist and World Champion Cyclist

Yvonne McGregor discovered competitive cycling relatively late in life, but soon made up for lost time. Her 1996 national 25-mile record of 51 minutes 50 seconds still stands.

Yvonne was born in a nursing home at Mornington Villas, Manningham, on 9 April 1961. Her father, Alan John, was a journalist with the *Yorkshire Post*, her mother Ray was a telephonist, also with the newspaper.

The family later moved from Manningham to Bradford Moor, where Yvonne attended Hanson Infant and Junior Schools, Pollard Park Middle and finally Carlton-Bolling Comprehensive School. In 1973, aged twelve, she joined Airedale and Spen Valley Athletic Club (now Bradford Airedale). Horsfall playing fields on Halifax Road became a regular venue, and she would train there three times a week with Sunday spent running through nearby Judy Woods.

When Yvonne left school the family moved to Perseverance Lane, Great Horton. Yvonne went to Ilkley College of Higher Education, and in 1979 qualified as a youth worker. Her first position was as a classroom assistant at Lindley House Special School, Bradford, and for the next few years Yvonne worked with special needs groups.

All her spare time was spent keeping fit, fell running and travelling. In 1983 she spent six months in Papua New Guinea and travelled overland through Malaysia, Thailand, Nepal and India. In 1988 she spent a month on a canoeing expedition with the Yorkshire Schools' Exploring Society as an assistant leader, circum-navigating the highest saltwater lake in the world, Lake Qinghai Hu, at 10,500ft, on the Tibetan plateau.

In 1989 Yvonne was eighth in the world fell-running championships, and in 1990 came eighteenth in the European long-dash course triathlon championships, which involved a 2,500-metre swim, an 80km ride and a half marathon. Now an accomplished fell runner and superb athlete, it was in 1990 aged twenty-nine that Yvonne went into cycling, a career that would bring her international acclaim.

Yvonne's first major breakthrough came in 1994 when she won a Common-wealth Games Gold Medal in the 25km race at Victoria. The following year she smashed the world hour record with a distance of 47.411km at Bogotá, Colombia. Her biggest disappointment came at the Atlanta Olympics in 1996 when she finished fourth in the 3,000-metre pursuit. In 2000 she capped her international career by taking the bronze medal at the Sydney Olympics, and then returned home to win the world pursuit championship in Manchester.

In domestic racing Yvonne has gained numerous national titles on both road and track. In 1993 she lowered the British 10-mile record to 21 minutes 15 seconds, beating Morley-born Beryl Burton's twenty-year-old time. In 1998 she moved to Cheshire to be closer to the velodrome in Manchester.

Despite being troubled by an ongoing back injury, she bowed out of international racing with a plucky fourth place in the world championships in Antwerp at the end of September 2001. In 2002 she was back in form when she broke the European hour record with 43.689km at the age of forty-one.

In December 2000 the Lord Mayor of Bradford, Councillor Stanley King, presented her with an engraved rose bowl at a civic reception. In 2001 Yvonne was awarded an MBE in the Queen's Birthday Honours List for services to cycling. She is a credit to her country, her sport, and her home town of Bradford.

Margaret McMillan CBE
Nursery School Pioneer

Bradford has the honour of being the pioneer city in the country in the field of child welfare. The first school medical inspections, first school meals and first school baths were all introduced to the country from this city. The achievement was due almost entirely to the efforts of one woman – Miss Margaret McMillan.

She was born in Westchester County near New York on 20 July 1860. Her parents were Scottish immigrants, but after the death of her father the family returned to Aberdeen. Her sister Rachel became the superintendent of a working girls' home in London, while Margaret travelled the continent as a student teacher.

Margaret then joined her sister in London. Her association with Bradford began with an invitation to lecture on 'socialist Rome', as it was then known in left-wing circles. Much of what she saw in the city appalled her. Many children were dirty, vermin infested, hungry and stunted. She arrived only to give a few lectures but these sights compelled her to stay. She joined the Independent Labour Party and for nearly ten years she worked among the poorest children in the city. From 1894 to 1902 she was a member of the Bradford School Board, the youngest ever to join and the first woman.

Throughout all this time she fought to improve the quality of education for the children of industrial workers. It was in 1897 that she gained her first victory for deprived children, opening the first school baths in the country at Wapping Street and Feversham Street schools. Green Lane School, Manningham, introduced the first school dinners in the country. The school's head at that time was Jonathan Priestley, father of the young J.B. Priestley.

Medical inspections were introduced when the city appointed its first health inspector for schools; the rest of the country would follow later. However, it was the open-air nursery movement that Margaret had founded with her sister Rachel for which she is best known. The first opened in Bradford, one in London followed. These schools were soon established throughout the country after the 1905 Education Act empowered local authorities to set them up.

In 1917 Margaret McMillan was given the CBE for her pioneering work. Later she founded the Rachel McMillan Training College for teachers, and one such college in Bradford was named after Margaret herself. She later described Bradford as 'the city of my heart'. She lived at 49 Hanover Square where a plaque was installed with the words 'All children were mine', with the dates during which she lived at the house, 1893–1902.

Margaret McMillan died after a short illness at a nursing home in Harrow-on-the-Hill, Middlesex, on 27 March 1931 aged seventy-one. She was buried at Brockley Cemetery in the same grave as her sister Rachel.

Leading Seaman James Magennis VC
Victoria Cross Recipient, Second World War

In July 1945 James Magennis, dressed in his naval frogman gear, swam from a midget submarine to plant limpet mines on the 10,000-ton Japanese cruiser *Takao* in the Johore Straits.

He was born in Belfast on 27 October 1919. After being refused by the Army he joined the Royal Navy and HMS *Kandahar*, a new destroyer, in November 1939 as an able seaman. Just before Christmas 1941 the ship hit a mine off Cap Bon, Tunisia. He was one of the survivors rescued by HMS *Jaguar*. After a few changes of vessel in October 1942 he received a mention in despatches for his part in a midget submarine attack on the German battleship *Tirpitz* as she lay heavily protected in a Norwegian fjord. He was then a member of the passage crew, which had to deliver the midget sub 1,000 miles from Britain to Norway. There was considerable difficulty in keeping the three-man craft below the surface and preventing it from diving below the 150ft safety margin. He said later that this was perhaps the most nerve-racking incident he had taken part in, more frightening even than the action that won him the Victoria Cross.

It was towards the end of the war that James Joseph Magennis's incredible valour was rewarded with Britain's highest award. The citation in the *London Gazette* of 13 November 1945 reads: 'On 31st July 1945 in the Johore Straits, leading seaman Magennis, a diver in the midget submarine XE.3, attached limpet mines to the Japanese Cruiser *Takao* under particularly difficult circumstances. He had to squeeze through a narrow space in the partly-open diving hatch, and then scrape barnacles off the bottom of the cruiser before attaching the limpets. During this time his breathing apparatus was leaking, and he returned to the submarine after completion of his task very exhausted. On withdrawing, his commander found that one of the limpet carriers which was being jettisoned would not release itself and Magennis immediately volunteered to free it; this he did after five minutes of nerve-racking work with a heavy spanner.' He was awarded the Victoria Cross by George VI at Buckingham Palace.

In the mid-1950s he became a resident of Bradford, living in Newton Street, West Bowling, and working as a television engineer. In 1962 he moved to Moser Crescent, Swain House estate, when he was made redundant and remained unemployed for 15 months. Asked if he was bitter that the bravery he showed in 1945 now seemed to count for little, he replied: 'People do not seem to think much of heroes these days, but I am not bitter, I do not want to moan or cry poverty, the country does not owe me a living. All my life I have worked hard and I would like to have the chance to do so again.' Later he was employed as chief service engineer for hi-fi equipment at Rank Wharfedale, Bradford.

James Magennis, Ulster's only Victoria Cross recipient, died in the Royal Halifax Infirmary on 12 February 1986.

Shahid Malik

Magician and Escapologist

In the world of magic and illusion Shahid Malik is regarded by many as Britain's most exciting magician, one who has a reputation for entertaining and mesmerising audiences around the globe. His unique style and presentation leave a lasting impression.

Shahid was born on 8 March 1954 in Karachi. By the time he was four the family had made the decision to leave Pakistan behind and move to Bradford in search of a better life. Their first home was 12 St Margaret's Terrace but they later moved to Dirkhill Road. He attended Grange Infants' School, then Grange Junior, and Princeville Junior High (his favourite), where he was a prefect, and finally Grange Boys' Grammar School.

He first developed an interest in magic aged twelve having seen the famous magician Ali Bongo on the children's television programme *Zokko*. From then on many hours were spent reading, practising card tricks and anything else he could find related to magic. School years passed into college years when Shahid studied at the Bradford College of Art and Design for a diploma course in interior design. All the time he continued practising his craft and dreaming up new ideas, hoping one day he could make a profession of his all-consuming hobby.

By now it was the early 1970s and at the age of eighteen he would spend his free evenings performing all over the Bradford area free of charge. He knew then that performing to a live audience was the only way to improve his style. So he eagerly accepted any opportunity afforded by talent competitions at local clubs, audition nights to promote local performers and college events. Eventually the big break came – his first professional paid booking, a children's Christmas party at Allerton Social Club for the grand sum of £5.

Persistence paid off, and gradually Shahid began to get the offers of work he needed. These may not have been the top-line bookings he longed for and they were certainly not enough to keep his parents off his back (he was still living at home) but over time he became a regular performer at the variety clubs of Batley and Wakefield. At last he got the chance to work with some top performers of the day, such as David Essex, The Supremes, Little & Large, Glen Campbell and Gene Pitney. At the same time he was developing his escape stunts, performing at outdoor events and shows across the country, attracting huge crowds and making quite a name for himself. So began a career that has now made him world famous.

He nearly drowned while appearing live on TV performing Houdini's tank escape, and has twice been almost killed performing the burning rope escape, once falling from 75ft and once from 12ft, which did just as much damage. Shahid was left with fractured ribs and a broken arm after being knocked unconscious from both falls. In 1975 he was almost burnt alive after performing the bonfire escape and spent three weeks in intensive care with second and third degree burns to his face, arms and back – but accidents are, fortunately, few and far between.

From Iceland to Bangkok, Egypt to India, Shahid has spent the last twenty-five years travelling the world and performing his sensational magic and escape stunts. He has been awarded the supreme accolade of Magician of the Year and is the holder of two world records for his death-defying escape stunts. He regularly appears on television and at Royal Command Performances, both at home and abroad. Shahid and his wife Lisa have reached heights rarely achieved in the world of magic and illusion.

Shahid Malik is possibly the finest escape artist in the world, following in the footsteps of his idol Houdini. It comes as no surprise that this gentleman of magic, who could live anywhere in the world, has a great love for his home city of Bradford, and still lives in its heart.

2nd Lt Thomas H.B. Maufe VC
Victoria Cross Recipient, First World War

Thomas Harold Broadbent Maufe was born in Ilkley on 6 May 1898, the youngest son of Mr F.B. Maufe, formerly of Warlbeck, Ilkley. He was educated at Ghyllroyd School, Ilkley, and later at Uppingham. Entering the Royal Military Academy at Woolwich in October 1915, he was commissioned in the Royal Garrison Artillery in May 1916, becoming a second lieutenant in the 124th Siege Battery. It was with this battery that Maufe won the Victoria Cross in Feuchy, France, on 4 June 1917.

The official announcement in the *London Gazette* on 2 August 1917 read: 'Under intense artillery fire this officer, on his own initiative, repaired unaided the telephone lines behind the forward and rear positions, thereby enabling his battery to immediately open fire on the enemy. He further saved what might have proved a most disastrous occurrence by extinguishing a fire in an advanced ammunition dump, caused by a heavy explosion, regardless of the risk he ran from the effects of gas shells which he knew were in the dump. By his great promptitude, resource, and entire disregard of his own personal safety, he set an exceptionally fine example to all ranks.'

At this time he had just passed his nineteenth birthday. He was then the youngest holder in the British Army of that most coveted honour. Lieutenant Maufe's medal was presented by King George V in 1917. Before the end of the war, he rose to the rank of major and was one of the youngest men in the Army to gain that rank, for it was not until 6 May 1919 that he reached his twenty-first birthday. Later he had the distinction of unveiling Ilkley's War Memorial.

It was during the Second World War that tragedy came to Captain Maufe. He and another member of the Ilkley Home Guard were killed instantly in a trench mortar explosion at Manor Farm, Blubberhouse Moor, on 28 March 1942. He was forty-three. By this time he was a director of Brown Muff & Co. Ltd, Bradford, and resided at Hillside, Wells Road, Ilkley. He is buried in Ilkley Cemetery.

Sir Douglas Mawson

Explorer and Geologist

Look on the back of an old Australian $100 note and you will find the face of Bradford-born explorer and geologist Sir Douglas Mawson. He was the leader of several expeditions that made important contributions to Antarctic exploration and research which afforded him an Adelaide state funeral in 1958.

Douglas Mawson was born on 5 May 1882 at 25 Shipley Fields Road, Frizinghall. When he was two his father William sold off his UK business interests and took his young family to Australia. Douglas graduated from Sydney University in engineering and science, and found a position with the University of Adelaide lecturing in petrology (the study of the origin and structure of rocks). His first chance to visit the Antarctic came in 1907 when he joined an expedition led by the British explorer Ernest Shackleton. The team was the first to climb to the top of Mount Erebus, Antarctica's active volcano, and the first to reach the magnetic South Pole, a round trip of 1,260 miles.

Mawson later led his own Australian Antarctic expedition which charted 2,000 miles of coast, but nearly cost him his life. He selected his team and in the ship *Aurora* they sailed over 1,000 miles of pack ice to the Antarctic coast. Their first job was to build a hut, which they named 'Home of the Blizzard' because of the high winds. From this camp in the spring of 1912 several parties of explorers set out on foot. Mawson left with two companions, Mertz and Ninnis, with dogs and sledges. Some time into the journey Mawson and Mertz, who were ahead, noticed that Ninnis was no longer following. Retracing their steps, they found his sled marks which led to a crevasse. Mawson and Mertz were now forced to turn back because Ninnis had taken with him to his death the best dogs in the expedition and some valuable equipment. The two men had to live on dog flesh, but soon Mertz began to show signs of illness. He died. Mawson buried him in the snow and went the last 100 miles towards base alone.

On his way back he too fell down a crevasse, but was saved by his sledge, which lodged above him, dangling on the end of the rope. He was tempted to slip off it and plunge to his death, but with great strength of mind he resisted, and finally hauled himself to safety. Mawson later reported that he felt the presence of a spirit at this time and it gave him the strength he needed to continue. He sawed his sled in half and dragged himself over more than 100 miles to reach the safety of the expedition base camp. He returned home to Australia to find himself a celebrity. In 1914 he was knighted and awarded the King's Polar Medal. Still a Professor of Geology at Adelaide University, he was to lead further Antarctic expeditions.

Often described as 'the modern Columbus', he never lost the longing for adventure. He died in Adelaide aged seventy-six on 15 October 1958 after a sudden illness.

Corporal Samuel Meekosha VC
Victoria Cross Recipient, First World War

It was on 19 November 1915 that Corporal Meekosha of the 1st/6th Battalion West Yorkshire Regiment (The Prince of Wales's Own) won the country's highest award for valour, the Victoria Cross.

Born in Leeds on 16 September 1893, Samuel Meekosha was the son of a Russian father and English mother. When the First World War broke out he enlisted as a member of the 1st/6th Battalion West Yorks at Belle Vue Barracks, Bradford, and with this local territorial battalion he went to France.

On 19 November 1915 near Yser in France Meekosha was in charge of a platoon of twenty NCOs and men, holding an isolated trench. During a heavy bombardment six of the men were killed, seven wounded and the remainder almost buried. The corporal scrambled out of the trench, helped by three unburied men, and set to work digging out his wounded and buried comrades in full view of the Germans. In spite of shells falling within 20 yards of them they managed to save the lives of four men, and this was reported in the *London Gazette* on 22 January 1916. Meekosha was the senior NCO and as a result he was awarded the Victoria Cross. His three comrades received the Distinguished Conduct Medal.

On leave in 1917, he returned to Bradford to marry a local girl, Bertha. Although wounded later in the right wrist and temple, he survived the war. In 1919 he joined the regular army and served as a captain with the corps of military accountants for seven years until it was disbanded in 1926. He then embarked on a career in civilian life, buying a wholesale tobacconist's business in Market Street, Bradford, while living at 288 Great Horton Road, but this business failed. Moving to Birmingham he took up a similar occupation, working as a representative for a tobacco company on commission only, hoping that his wife and children could follow him when he had a more permanent position.

When the Second World War began, he immediately made himself available for service. He was accepted in the Royal Army Ordnance Corps, promoted to major, and performed a valuable role in Lincolnshire. It was at this time that he changed his name to Ingham; this was to avoid the limelight of his Victoria Cross which was more evident in wartime. He achieved the obscurity that he had desired.

After the war he worked for some years for the John Player Tobacco Company. He died at his home in Blackwood, Monmouthshire, on 8 December 1950 aged fifty-seven.

Emmanuel 'Manny' Mercer
Champion Jockey

It must be unique that two brothers born in a city not renowned for the Sport of Kings should become household names as champion jockeys, alongside the greats like Sir Gordon Richards, Charlie Smirke, Doug Smith and Joe Sime, the riders who dominated British racing in the second half of the twentieth century.

Emmanuel 'Manny' Mercer was born in 1930 in Lingard Street off Bolton Road, Bradford, and was the eldest son of a family of eight. His father worked for many years for Butterfield Tank Works in Shipley.

Manny attended Lilycroft and Drummond Road Schools. Leaving school at fifteen he spent two years at Lister's Mill, Manningham, in the spinning department as a bobbin ligger (a worker who removes the full bobbins from the spinning frame and 'ligs' or lays empty bobbins on the frame for refilling). He was so small he had trouble reaching the bobbin rail.

Because he was so small it was hinted that he should be a jockey and Manny approached the Youth Employment Bureau in Bradford to see whether this career might be open to him. The bureau seems to have been quite successful in finding postitions for boys with this calling and it was not long before Manny had a job as a stable boy at Mablethorpe.

He soon progressed from stable boy to apprentice jockey, and joined George Colling at Newmarket. He first made headlines when he brought a 100–1 outsider called Jockey Treble home to win the 1947 Lincolnshire Handicap. He was soon to become the idol of the racing fraternity and looked like becoming another Gordon Richards.

In 1951 he won the Cesarewitch on Three Cheers. In 1952 he rode in the USA and in the same year was runner-up to Len Hutton for Sportsman of the Year. In 1953 he won the 1,000 Guineas, and in 1954 he wore the Queen's colours at Epsom.

In 1959 he was ranked among the six best jockeys in the world, but it was in September that year that Manny was tragically killed, aged twenty-nine, at Ascot, when he was unseated from his mount Priddy Fair before the start of the Red Deer Stakes.

Manny's untimely death meant he had only half a career. What further races and records he may have won can only be speculation, but it is clear he would have stayed at the top.

Joe Mercer OBE

Champion Jockey

Joe, like his brother Manny, was born in Lingard Street on 25 October 1934. It was in Victor Road in the shadow of Lister's Mill, Manningham, that Joe spent his early years. Like Manny he attended Lilycroft and Drummond Road Schools until he was nine and the family moved to Cheadle, Cheshire.

Because he was small like his brother and had a love of racing it was inevitable that he should follow in Manny's footsteps. He became an apprentice jockey at the age of twelve and rode his first winner when he was sixteen, a horse called Eldoret at Bath in 1950. Joe rode his first classic winner at the age of eighteen on Ambiguity in The Oaks in 1953.

In 1979 he was crowned Champion Jockey with 164 winners, 22 more than his nearest rival, the previous champion Willie Carson, and in 1980 Mercer was awarded the OBE for his services to racing.

Joe went on the become one of Britain's best-loved riders, retiring in fine style in 1985 after riding Bold Rex to win the November Handicap at Doncaster at 20–1. In all he had ridden 2,810 winners in this country, his most famous and favourite being Brigadier Gerard whom he rode in 17 of his 18 wins. He also rode Highclere for the Queen, winning the 1,000 Guineas and the Prix de Diane.

Over his thirty-five years in the saddle, Joe had eight Classic wins, which made him the fourth most successful jockey in the country behind Lester Piggott, Sir Gordon Richards and Doug Smith. On retirement Joe became a jockeys' agent before taking up a post at Gainsborough Stud, where he is racing manager to Sheikh Maktoum al Maktoum and his racing associates.

Gertie Millar

Music Hall and Comedy Actress

Gertie Millar was one of the most brilliant stars of musical comedy, when musical comedy was at its best. She found the road to success but worked hard for it; she always had one goal in sight, to become a great star. Her life story reads like a fairy tale – from the back streets of Bradford she moved on to entertain royalty as the Dowager Countess of Dudley at Himley Hall.

Gertie was born Gertrude Millar on 20 February 1879 at 21 Grimwith Street, a cul-de-sac off Carlisle Road, near the junction with Whetley Hill, Bradford. The family later moved to a house in the neighbourhood of Drewton Street. Her home was near Christ Church School where she was educated. By all accounts she was an exemplary pupil, tall, slim and attractive with dark hair and large limpid eyes.

She also lived near the Theatre Royal, which was to influence her whole career. John Hart, the producer who made pantomimes featuring boys and girls, selected Gertie to appear in the 1891/2 production of *Red Riding Hood*. She was then in her twelfth year. After the close of the pantomime she secured concert engagements with Walter Holmes at the Mechanics' Institute, St George's Hall and many other halls in the area. In the 1892/3 pantomime season she was engaged as the girl babe in a Manchester production of *Babes in the Wood*. By this time she was making a reputation for herself and was being billed as a juvenile comedienne. She was only fourteen when she joined the Arthur Brogden Company, which gave her an engagement which lasted six years. At the end of that time she was back in pantomime in Bradford and so well established as a principal that she had reached London, where she played Dandini in *Cinderella*. By 1901 she had reached the Gaiety Theatre in the West End where she remained for seven years.

It was at the Theatre Royal, Bradford, that the romance of her life began. At twenty-one she was playing in the touring production of the *Messenger Boy* and in the audience was Lionel Monckton, who was later to compose *The Arcadians* and many other successful musicals. Monckton was bowled over by her talent, and by the girl herself. Their romance was a whirlwind one and within weeks they were married.

At the end of this period she went to New York and succeeded as Mitza in *The Girls of Gottenberg* but was soon back at the Gaiety and Daly's. During the next decade, she appeared in many musicals, pantomimes and tours. *The Orchid* ran for 559 performances, *The Quaker Girl* for 556 performances, and *The Dancing Mistress* for 241, a phenomenal achievement, which gave her success until the middle of the First World War. As war raged people's tastes changed. They were now flocking to the comfort of the new cinema palaces rather than the music halls and theatres.

Gertie practically retired in 1917; she made her last appearance on stage at the Alhambra when she starred at the head of a variety bill. She finally retired in 1918. She always retained the love of her home town and gave generously to many charities, including holidays for poor children and donations to the new Royal Infirmary in Duckworth Lane.

In 1924 her husband died and some months later she married William Humble Ward, the second Earl of Dudley. Before the war he had been Governor-General of Australia. The working-class Bradford girl who grew up to be one of the best-loved stars and most photographed women of the Edwardian era had become the Countess of Dudley.

The union between the Earl and the Countess only lasted eight years, for he died in 1932. Gertrude chose to stay in France after she was widowed, and returned to Britain after the outbreak of the Second World War. She outlived the Earl by twenty years and passed away at her home in Chiddingford, Surrey, in April 1952 aged seventy-three.

Austin Mitchell

Member of Parliament and Television Journalist

Austin Mitchell's family emerged from the moorland mists around Heptonstall where they were handloom weavers in the eighteenth century. In the 1840s they moved down to Halifax to work in Ackroyd's Mill, and in the twentieth century the family finally settled in Baildon, where Austin was born on 19 March 1934.

From the family home on the new Ferniehurst Estate in Lower Baildon and wearing his clogs, Austin went to Woodbottom Council School. Aged nine he sat the County Minor examination and got into Bingley Grammar School, which gave him a wonderful education. Baildon was its own little world where life centred on chapels, churches and the cricket club. He was sent to Charlestown Methodist Church every Sunday, signed the pledge and took part in the annual *Messiah*. He transferred to St John's Church because they had Scouts and Cubs (9th Shipley), which he loved. Baildon was 'a great place to grow up', so close to the moors, the woods, the rivers and Tong Park Dam with their great opportunities to catch frogs and minnows in jam jars. Outings to Bradford were the focal point for shopping, books and entertainment – the New Victoria, its dances and the Bradford Jazz Club in the Castle Hotel, featuring Bennie Netherwood and the Wool City Jazzmen. 'It was a wonderful world to grow up in.'

At fifteen he applied for a job at Baildon Combing, but they deemed him unemployable. So he stayed at school and drifted to Manchester University on a State Scholarship, and then to Oxford University where he gained an MA and a DPhil ('largely unused!'). He went to New Zealand, the only part of the world prepared to offer him a job, he says. He then came back to Oxford on a fellowship, but was so bored that when he sat next to Geoffrey Cox at a college dinner and Cox offered him a job at the newly born Yorkshire Television, Austin accepted immediately. He arrived the next day to find all the staff on strike. He was employed at £12 per day, shortly raised to £12.50 with a free Metro Pass to cover the cost of travel from Shipley to Leeds.

93

He held the YTV job for eight years, during which time people used to ask, whenever he went out with Richard Whiteley, 'Who's that ugly bugger with Austin?' Now, Austin says, it's the other way round: 'Who's that geriatric slavering old sod wi' that lovely young lad Richard?'

In 1977 'I made the mistake of going into politics!' (He told his mother he was going to prison and she was much happier that way.) He was elected MP for Grimsby where, he said, 'they hate Yorkshire folk', so he pretended he was from New Zealand!

He says he has tried to raise the intellectual level of politics by writing two Yorkshire joke books and a lot of stuff about how wonderful Yorkshire was when he 'wor a lad', before 'London and its financial interests ruined our industries, strangled our proud cities, counties and generally drained the life out of us to enrich themselves. Thank heavens we're still God's Own People in God's Own County.'

A former Parliamentary Private Secretary, Opposition Whip, member of the Treasury Select Committee, Civil Service Select Committee and Front Bench Spokesperson on Trade and Industry, he currently sits on the Agriculture Select Committee.

Dennis Mitchell

International Professional Wrestler

Dennis Mitchell was a professional wrestler from the late 1940s, and represented Britain when Bradford was a major force in international wrestling. He held British, European and Commonwealth titles at various weights including heavyweight, and was known as 'Golden Boy' to his many fans.

Born on 11 August 1929, he attended Princeville Junior and Secondary School in Listerhills. He was shy and had difficulty in speaking, so when ridiculed by other kids he hit back with his fists. At eight he started boxing at the Bradford City Boys Club, and could soon beat boys of fifteen and sixteen. At one time he ran away from home to join a boxing booth and travelled round the fairs challenging all comers, fighting as many as fifteen times a day for coins which were thrown into the ring.

When National Service came he joined the Royal Marines. During this time, 1948–50, he was the champion inter-regiment marksman and swimmer with 45 Commando. On returning from the forces he joined Norman Morrell's gymnasium and trained alongside wrestlers of the calibre of Norman Walsh, Les Kellett and Eric Taylor. In those days Bradford was known as the wrestlers' city.

It was in Germany that he made his name, wrestling as OK1. In three years he never lost a fight and gained a tremendous following. They even struck 10,000 medallions bearing his face at the mint in Munich. He was the only wrestler to have been given this honour. In his twelve years at the top, he met millionaires, maharajahs, sheikhs and barons, and travelled the world over.

He retired from the sport in 1975, and became increasingly involved with children's charities, including UNICEF. He stood as a Labour candidate for Bradford Council at Odsal, became Markets Chairman for the Council (there is a monument at the entrance of the new market stall section dedicated to him) and served as the Chairman of Bradford Water Board, seeing it through to private control.

He was a publican at the Fairweather Green pub from 1975 to 1978, a demolition contractor until 1988 and then took other security work until 1992. He remained fit until 1997 when he was taken ill.

After a long illness he was transferred to Manorlands, Haworth, and died on 29 October 1997, aged sixty-eight. After a funeral service at St Wilfrid's CE Church, Lidget Green, he was buried at Scholemoor Cemetery on 11 November.

Dennis is remembered as a wrestler's wrestler, a gentleman, having a deep love for his family, and as a hard worker for good causes, especially those that helped children, a man with no airs and graces.

Albert Modley

Comedian

Yorkshire comedian Albert Modley was loved and admired in his own county. He was born in Liverpool in 1902 but his family moved to Barnsley, then Ilkley, where he attended Ilkley National School.

Albert's first job was working as a grocer's boy, then butcher's assistant, where he learnt to ride the delivery horses. His father trained him to be a physical training instructor, and he won the amateur boxing championship of Yorkshire in 1917. Quite the athlete, he was also a Wharfedale diving champion, but he did not earn a living from sport and took a job in the parcels department at Forster Square station in Bradford. During the General Strike in 1926 he launched his career in local clubland in a double act with fellow railwayman Eddie Totty, and it was said that they entertained at almost every pub in Bradford.

Albert said when he went into show business 'it was the railway's gain not loss', being the first to admit his tomfoolery caused many disruptions with management, staff and customers.

He first came to national prominence as 'Our Enoch' the never-do-anything-right little man with the plaintive voice, who was a character in Harry Korris's peak hour radio show *Happidrome* during the 1930s, a show that captured the attention of the nation during the Second World War.

He never told a dirty joke and was renowned for his kindness. Daft antics and yarns were his speciality. He always wore a cap on stage and was able to observe every echo of humour that came out of the vast caverns of the northern region. Albert was superb in pantomime. Francis Laidler of the Bradford Alhambra had noted this at an early stage, and cast Albert as the star in thirteen of his extravaganzas at the Alhambra and Leeds Royal theatres.

He also made films, notably *Up for the Cup, Take Me to Paris, Bob's Your Uncle*, and *Bob's Shop*, but it was on the stage that Albert excelled. Perhaps most people will remember his famous tram driver's sequence where he would stand and squat, pretending to be a tram driver using a large drum and cymbals to imitate the controls, juddering his body and calling to some imaginary person on the line to 'get out of the way'.

After many years topping the bill in music hall, pantomimes and summer seasons, Albert was still around show business and became popular with a second generation in the new great club boom of the 1960s.

For many years Albert had lived in Morecambe, which had taken him to its heart, so much so that he was granted the freedom of the town. He died on 23 February 1979 aged seventy-seven and his remains are buried at Morecambe Crematorium.

Adrian Moorhouse MBE
Olympic Gold Medal Swimmer

Adrian Moorhouse, a modest man, set his sights on athletic greatness, and achieved it in 1988 with a gold medal at the Seoul Olympics.

Adrian was born at St Luke's Hospital, Bradford, on 24 May 1964 when the family lived in Nab Wood, Shipley. His first school was Victoria Preparatory in Saltaire, and then, aged seven, he went to Bradford Grammar School.

He learnt to swim at Aireborough Pool in Guiseley and then aged eleven Adrian joined the swimming club (Beacon Barracudas) which used the old Windsor Baths in Bradford. It was also the venue for his first Bradford Schools Championship races. He became a good district swimmer and joined the Bradford Schools squad. All the good swimmers from local schools joined the training squad and trained in many of the pools around Bradford.

Adrian swam with the Bradford Schools Team up to the age of fifteen (in 1979) when he left to join the Leeds Central team. This began his 'dual identity' – one foot in Bradford and the other in Leeds. For three years he would wake up in Bradford, go swimming in Leeds, back to school in Bradford, then after school over to Leeds to swim, and then return to Bradford to sleep.

Leaving school at eighteen, he won a year's swimming scholarship to the University of California, Berkeley. Now a Great Britain and England senior international, the records came thick and fast.

In 1982 Adrian won a gold medal in the 100-metre breaststroke event at the Brisbane Commonwealth Games. In 1983 he took European bronze in the 200 metres breaststroke and a silver in the 100 metres breaststroke. He was a finalist in the Olympic Games in Los Angeles in 1984 and in 1985 he took gold in the European Championships in the 100 metres breaststroke and recorded the best time in the world at that distance. In the 1986 Commonwealth Games he took gold in the 200 metres breaststroke and set a new European record at the World Championships. He made the world's best time in the 100-metre breaststroke in 1987 and took gold in the same event at the European Championships, and it was in the same year that he was awarded the MBE for services to sport. In 1988 his greatest achievement was to win gold in the 100-metres breaststroke at the Seoul Olympic Games. In 1989 at the European Championships in Bonn he again won gold for the 100-metres breaststroke, in world record time. In the 1992 Olympic Games in Barcelona he reached the final.

Shortly after the Olympic Games in Barcelona, he moved to London where he now has his own consultancy business, Lane 4. In 1989 he was awarded an honorary degree from Bradford University.

Sir Ken Morrison CBE

Chairman and Managing Director of Morrisons Supermarkets

When Sir Ken Morrison took over from his father William as head of the family business fifty-odd years ago, it consisted of a few market stalls and a handful of shops. The story since then has been of inexorable growth from the opening of the family's first supermarket in Bradford in 1961, through thirty-six years of unbroken sales and profit growth since the company was floated on the Stock Exchange in 1967.

Ken Morrison was born in 1931 when the family lived at 59 Lister Avenue, West Bowling. He attended Lorne Street Primary School, and in 1943 went on to Bradford Grammar School.

The firm was started in 1899 by his parents William and Hilda Morrison, who sold eggs and butter from stalls in Bradford and Dewsbury markets. As a boy Ken, the youngest of six children, helped out on the stalls in Rawson and John Street markets. During the Second World War the main stall in Rawson Market was destroyed by enemy bombing. One of his jobs was to help his father candle the eggs (hold them under candlelight to check their quality), and he was also general delivery boy.

Leaving school in 1950 he worked briefly for the firm before his National Service. While serving in Germany with the Royal Army Ordnance Corps, he received a call from his mother. She said his father was ill and asked him whether he wanted to keep the family business going. He decided to give it a try and returned from his National Service to run the grocery stall in Rawson Market. So, in 1952, at the age of twenty, he took over the business.

It was his brother-in-law Ken Blundell who brought the idea of self-service stores back from Canada after the war but kept the idea under his hat for the next few years. Later, in 1958, the two men mulled the idea over, took a gamble, and converted a double-fronted shop in James Street to include three specialist stalls, with three checkouts. The first self-service store in Bradford was born.

In 1961 Morrison converted the disused Victoria cinema, Girlington, into a supermarket. The rent for the building was £1,100 per annum. The shop took £1 million at the tills in the first year and for the first time customers could buy all their requirements under one roof – and there was ample car parking space.

His first custom-built supermarket was at Bolton Junction. In 1967 the company went public as William Morrison Supermarkets plc. The year 1977 saw his first supermarket outside West Yorkshire open in Ripon. In 1980 Farmers Boy Ltd began trading as a wholly owned subsidiary with a factory producing beef, pork, pizzas, cheese and bacon packing. In October 1987 Enterprise 5, a combination of industrial and commercial operations with a flagship superstore, was opened on the old International Harvesters site at Five Lane Ends.

Today the company has 119 supermarkets generating an annual turnover of £3.9 billion. Sir Ken's retailing philosophy has remained the same for decades. It is simple. He prefers to shun what the company calls the 'hype and gimmickry' of rivals – such as loyalty cards – in favour of 'no nonsense low price offers'. He is regarded as a grandee of the British grocery business and still walks the shop floors. In 2004 Morrisons acquired the Safeway chain of supermarkets.

While his mother lived to see his first few supermarkets open, his father died when Ken was twenty-four. He was awarded the CBE in 1990 and knighted in 2000 in the New Year's Honours List.

Bryan Mosley

Actor

Like most 'soap' actors Bryan Mosley had a good grounding in the conventional theatre.

Bryan Mosley was born in Leeds on 25 August 1931 but he and his family were to live in Shipley for over thirty years. After he completed his National Service in the RAF, an officer suggested he take up acting. Training at the Esmé Church Northern Theatre School, Bradford, gave him confidence and wide experience of rep in the north of England. But television was to be his forte and he was in on the ground floor when the medium began expanding as a vehicle for serious and popular drama from the 1950s onward. He was in a number of *Armchair Theatre* and *Play of the Week* productions.

He spent thirty-seven years in *Coronation Street* as Alf Roberts, and became one of its longest-serving actors. He also featured in other television hits such as *Z Cars*, *The Saint* and *Doctor Who*, and a number of films including *Far from the Madding Crowd* (1967), *A Kind of Loving* (1962) and *Charlie Bubbles* (1967). In *Get Carter* (1971) he displayed memorably sinister qualities as a Newcastle thug who threatens the protagonist Michael Caine, until Caine throws him off a car park roof.

But 1961 launched him into the role with which he became totally identified in the public mind for many years. Alf Roberts became one of television's most famous shopkeepers, serving twice as Mayor of Weatherfield, once with the Rovers Return landlady Annie Walker as his Lady Mayoress. Bryan survived the trials and tribulations of the many storylines of *Coronation Street* until a number of health scares contributed to his leaving the street. In his last appearance he died of a heart attack in an armchair just as the clock struck midnight on New Year's Eve. Ironically, it was a heart attack that was to kill Bryan just weeks after his final episode was shown.

He received an honorary degree from Bradford University. He died at Shipley on 9 February 1999.

Frank Newbould

Poster Artist

Frank Newbould was one of the most successful poster designers of modern times, and his bold colourful railway posters did much to relieve the gloom of many of Britain's underground stations.

Frank was born on 24 September 1887 at the family home, 174 Lumb Lane, Manningham. His father John Matthew was a chemist and druggist with a shop near the Theatre Royal in Bradford. Frank attended the local preparatory school in Manningham and aged ten went to Bradford Grammar School.

After leaving school, he studied at the Bradford School of Art. His first known work may be an advertisement for Vimant Gas Mantles of Bradford in 1909; it is possible that this was carried out while he was studying in Bradford. When he left the art school he was employed as head of the art

department at Lund Humphries & Co. Ltd, publishers.

In 1913 he moved to London to study at the Camberwell School of Art, where he won the Board of Education bronze and silver medals for poster work, and took first-class honours for design. After the First World War Frank was known for his black-and-white work and was regarded as an excellent exponent of what could be achieved with a 'J' nib.

Following the amalgamation of the railway companies in 1923, each of the four companies (GWR, LMSR, LNER and SR) developed its own style and identity. The Southern Railway used cheerful characters to promote the holiday resorts it served; the Great Western emphasised the speed and efficiency of its service; the LNER developed a uniform standard and continuity of design, where the emphasis was on the destination, presented in graphically interesting works.

From 1926 to 1931 under the leadership of William Teasdale, Frank was one of five poster artists working exclusively for the LNER. Like most of his peers who produced work for railway companies, Frank was primarily a commercial artist and he was known for his businesslike methods. A visitor to his studio in

Kensington in 1925 described him as 'the most business-like artist I have ever come across. Frank is a businessman: you can't get away from it.' His guiding principle in setting out on a new piece of work was 'Will it sell the goods?' and he had this question prominently pinned up on his studio notice-board.

His cartoons proved an attractive feature at the Ideal Homes Exhibition for many years. To obtain material for his designs he constantly visited continental Europe and America, and travelled as far as Trinidad. In 1938 he was elected a fellow of the Royal Society of Art.

During the Second World War the Railway Executive Committee was keen to discourage non-essential use of the railway network. Much of the poster work produced in those years was practical in nature and was based on slogans such as 'Is your journey really necessary?' As the war progressed, however, the pictorial poster re-emerged. In 1942 Frank joined the War Office and worked as an assistant to Abram Games, where he designed a series of pictorial posters with the slogan 'Your Britain: Fight for it Now'. He also designed posters for the GWR, Orient Line, White Star Line and Belgian Railways.

He was known for his use of bold and vibrant colour. One writer described seeing his poster for the White Star Line of New York 'with the Telephone building in red and the Woolworth building in white behind it', and declared that he felt for the first time the desire to visit that city to see its architecture. Frank's poster work is still shown and collected around the world; one of his best known is of Cruden Bay, the LNER-created hotel and golf resort of the Aberdeenshire coast. This image is particularly favoured by golf aficionados.

One of Bradford's most prolific and renowned artists, whose beautiful posters once adorned our many railway stations, Frank Newbould died at the age of sixty-four at his home in Kensington in 1951.

Monsignor John O'Connor
The Original Father Brown

Father Brown appears to be the simplest, dullest character imaginable as a dabbler in the world of the mystery detective. But he had an uncanny understanding of human nature and was able to get into the mind of the criminal.

Monsignor O'Connor became 'Father Brown' some time after his first meeting with the author G.K. Chesterton in 1904. They were introduced at a house in Keighley and walked over the moors to Ilkley together.

Monsignor O'Connor had with him his huge umbrella, his little brown paper parcels and his hat, and it was these features that Chesterton noted. He built his famous character upon them but it was not until two years after the first Father Brown book was published that Monsignor O'Connor knew he had been portrayed as a clerical detective.

John O'Connor was born at Clonmel, County Tipperary, on 5 December 1870. He came to Bradford in 1898 after training for the priesthood at Douai, France, and the English College in Rome. He was for a time assistant headmaster at St Bede's Grammar School, spent three years at Keighley, a year in Leeds and was parish priest at Heckmondwike from 1905 to 1919. From there he came to St Cuthbert's, Manningham. Monsignor O'Connor was quite a distinguished writer himself and published a collection of his sermons. He was also a renowned collector of art, and had some thirty-nine paintings. These were sold at Sotheby's in 1950 for £1,600.

Sadly there were no royalties for Monsignor O'Connor from the Father Brown stories which are still sold in large quantities throughout the world. Father Brown was also introduced to the world of film and television: in 1954 Columbia Pictures produced a film entitled *Father Brown*, starring Alec Guinness in the title role. In 1974 Anglia Television produced their first *Father Brown* series, starring Kenneth More as the detective, and others have followed.

Monsignor O'Connor remained at St Cuthbert's Church until 1952, probably smiling to himself many times and remembering the walk nearly half a century earlier with G.K. Chesterton across Ilkley Moor. This *Father Brown* never solved a crime in his life – he had never tried. He was, however, every inch a character, a man of many talents with a sparking humour. Monsignor O'Connor died at St Joseph's Nursing Home, Horsforth, aged eighty-one, on 6 February 1952 and was buried on the 11th at Scholemoor Cemetery, Bradford.

Oliver Onions
Novelist

One of the great writers of supernatural fiction was born in Bradford. His name was Oliver Onions. A contemporary of J.B. Priestley, Onions wrote some of the finest ghost stories of the time.

Oliver Onions was born on 3 July 1873 at 37 Ripon Street, Undercliffe, and later lived at St James Square, Manchester Road, and in Ann Place, Horton Lane. He attended Feversham Street Higher Grade Board School and afterwards Bradford Grammar School. In the evenings he attended classes as a student at the Technical College, but always contended that most of his learning came from his father's bookshelves. At seventeen he went to London to study at the National Art Training School in South Kensington. He also spent time in Paris where he edited a student periodical.

For a while he was an apprentice to Robert Eagle, the well-known Well Street printer to whom he was always permanently grateful for his patience and indulgence. Taking up a career in art, he illustrated books, worked as a draughtsman in a printing office, designed posters and was a war artist for a magazine during the South African War.

After starting work as a journalist and artist he turned to novel writing. (He later changed his name to George Oliver Onions but reverted to the name with which he was christened after deciding it was better for a novelist.) He had some forty novels published which were of outstanding interest to West Riding people, for in them he embodied autobiographical details and memories of his early years in Bradford, presenting an authentic picture of life as it was lived there in the 1880s and 1890s.

He was a slow worker, rewriting as many times as he considered necessary to achieve perfection, and was scrupulous about detail, going far as to take trips by air or perform chemical experiments to be sure of accuracy in describing them.

He is best remembered for his talent in writing ghost stories. His tales of the supernatural are found in four collections *Back o' the Moon* (1906), *Widdershins* (1911), *Ghosts in Daylight* (1924) and *The Painted Face* (1929). These were brought together as *The Collected Ghost Stories of Oliver Onions* in 1935. Many of his works are still widely collected today. As a writer of the supernatural he was not bettered by any other author of his time.

The Bradford novelist died at Aberystwyth on 9 April 1961 aged eighty-seven.

Doug Padgett
Yorkshire and England Cricketer

Rosy-faced and determined, Doug Padgett was a neat, orthodox batsman of average height (5ft 9in), equally at home opening or in the middle order.

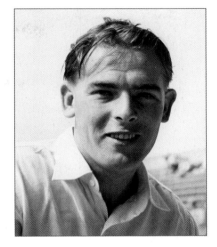

Douglas Ernest Vernon Padgett was born on 20 July 1934 at St Luke's Hospital. The family lived in Arthur Street, Idle. He first attended Idle Church School, and later Thorpe Secondary Modern, also in Idle. Leaving school at fifteen, he was employed at a stationery business in Leeds Road, Bradford, but feeling that he needed something more secure, he went to Joseph Dawson's wool combers as an apprentice wool sorter.

Doug came from a cricketing family; his father and elder brother played for Idle. It was here that he learnt his cricket. He became the youngest batsman to play in the Bradford League at the age of thirteen and he was a few days short of his sixteenth birthday when he appeared for Yorkshire seconds against Northumberland at Thirsk in the Minor Counties competition. In 1951 he became Yorkshire's youngest debutant, aged 16 years and 321 days, a record he held for thirty years until nudged into second place by Paul Jarvis (16 years 75 days).

In 1952 he was called up for National Service, joining the Royal Signals at Catterick as a physical training instructor. He continued playing cricket both at home and the Army Combined Services; 1954 found him back in civvy street. He was soon a permanent member of probably the best-known and most successful Yorkshire team ever.

His contribution to Yorkshire can be measured by the fact that he played in seven championship-winning sides. As a number 3 batsman, he was a dapper, neat right-hander, with an exemplary technique. His 21,124 first-class runs made him one of Yorkshire's twelve greatest scorers. In all, he hit 29 first-class centuries and completed 1,000 runs in each of twelve seasons, with one really outstanding achievement in 1959 when he scored 2,158 runs.

In 1960 he was selected to play in two Test Matches against South Africa – one at Old Trafford and the final Test at the Oval. In 1960/1 he toured to New Zealand with the young MCC party. In 1971 after a twenty-year first-team career with Yorkshire, he decided to close the chapter. He took over as second team captain, later becoming the chief club coach.

His retirement as coach in 1999 brought to a close a remarkable span of over half a century of active cricketing service. A very modest man, with outstanding personal achievements, he was a real Yorkshire stalwart. He was also a handy right-arm medium pace bowler. When questioned about this, he replied, with true Yorkshire relish, 'I only got to bowl when the matches were lost!'

Pat Paterson

Actress

On 25 August 1978 Charles Boyer, the world-renowned screen actor, was sorting out papers and getting his house in neat order. His wife of forty-four years, Patricia, had died and was being buried on this day. The following day he took a fatal overdose of barbiturates, only two days before his seventy-ninth birthday, to be with his beloved Patricia, alias Pat Paterson, formerly of Bradford.

Patricia Paterson was her real name, and she was born at 15 Round Street, West Bowling, Bradford, on 7 April 1911. The Patersons were a lower middle-class family and Pat's father was a wool merchant. She was Patricia only within her family circle; to everyone else she was Patsy or Patty.

Her mother, seeking to capitalise on Patricia's aggressive charm and blonde cuteness, pushed her on to the stage at an early age. She loved everything about the stage and had dancing lessons, starting with tap at the age of five and ballet at eight. Before she was ten Pat had joined the *Babes in the Wood* pantomime, staying in the Bradford production for five years. Because she was boy crazy her father removed her from the show, but Pat ran away from home with a boy from the company. It was only years later that she was reconciled with her family.

Deserted in London by her boyfriend and left to her own devices, she got work in a third-rate music hall. She was good, and at seventeen she won a spot in a West End review called *Stop Flirting*, graduating from chorus to feature roles. She also moved into British pictures when the 'talkies' came in.

By the time she was twenty-two she was a well-known player, if not quite a star, with her own growing fan club, but only in England. She then appeared in a film called *Bitter Sweet* that was screened in the USA. Fox's Robert Kane believed that Pat had stolen the show and signed her up, which required no coaxing, as almost every player in British films coveted nothing so much as a ticket to Hollywood, a standard contract being seven years at $500 per week.

Her first Hollywood film was *Bottom's Up* in 1934 with Spencer Tracy. She went on to appear in seven more movies, including *Charlie Chan in Egypt* in 1935.

She had always enjoyed the company of men and in England had rejected one proposal after another because her career came first. Then at a studio party she bumped into Charles Boyer. Her only disappointment was that he had never heard of her – but she had never heard of him either! They were married three weeks later.

Pat and her husband were devoted to each other during their forty-four years of marriage, and there was never any hint of indiscretion or infidelity. A movie icon, Charles Boyer took the stage with the likes of Greta Garbo, Katherine Hepburn and Ingrid Bergman, but the love of his life was a slim blonde girl from West Bowling. Charles and Pat are buried side by side at Holy Cross Cemetery, Culver City, Los Angeles.

Edward Peel

Actor

Edward Peel's reliability and conscientiousness as an actor have led him to be cast in one production after another, in films, on stage and on TV in everything from Shakespeare to *Emmerdale*.

Born on 10 December 1943 at 27 Clara Road, Bolton Villas, he attended Swain House Nursery and Primary Schools. He was in both Cubs and Scouts at Bolton Villas Congregational Church and spent the long hot summers in the childhood pursuits of cricket, hopscotch and tin can squat.

From primary school he went to Belle Vue Grammar School, later attending Bradford Training College during which he spent a short spell teaching at St Augustine's Primary School in Otley Road. During this time he had joined the Green Room evening classes, learning about all aspects of theatre before moving to the local Amateur Group Theatre Organisation in Westgate, Bradford, and progressing to the Bradford Civic Playhouse.

Edward, a busy stage, television and film actor, has played numerous 'heavies' on television over the years, from the original portrayal of Jackie's jailbird father in *Emmerdale* to, later in the same series, Anthony Cairns. Earlier parts had been in *Juliet Bravo* as Chief Inspector Perrin, and in BBC TV's *Doctor Who* series where he was voted the 'Best Villain or Monster' for his chilling performance as Kane, the galactic criminal in the 'Dragonfire' episode of the science fiction favourite.

A remarkable list of appearances shows the versatility of this in-demand actor from *Cracker*, *Casualty*, and more recently as Station Officer John Coleman in the long-running series *London's Burning*. All this, and tours with the Royal Shakespeare Company!

Edward joins the number of theatre people who have come out of the Bradford Civic Playhouse to became household names. Being listed as a 'top villain', however, takes place in the realm of make-believe. In real life you could not find a more likeable man, who now lives with his family in a small Lincolnshire coastal town.

John Pennington

Entrepreneur

John Pennington is a true Bradford patriot and if he had been born 150 years ago he would probably have been one of Bradford's well-known aldermen or perhaps even its mayor. With his modern approach and a true love of the city's heritage, he has a vision and hope that Bradford 'may soon be on the right track'.

Born on 21 February 1949 at 268 Bradford Road, Frizinghall, he attended Miss Altoft's Preparatory School in Nab Wood. Failing the entrance exam for Bradford Grammar School, he went to Fulneck Moravian School, Pudsey, which gave him an idea of what life was all about, but he left with no qualifications other than three O-levels.

Bradford at that time was full of art students, but John did not wish to pursue that route. Instead he went to Bradford College for two years and gained a diploma in textiles, which enabled him to join the family business, the Bradford Wool Auctions, at its offices in the Mechanics' Institute building. When the Mechanics was demolished, the business moved to the still vibrant Wool Exchange. When the wool trade went into decline in the 1980s the business moved to Shipley.

John's interest in show business developed when he became a disc jockey in the late 1960s, working at the new Elmer discotheque in Shipley. He soon had a vast knowledge of the disc jockeying methods which were taking every city by storm. He was in great demand, performing at the many Mecca clubs, Radio Royal (at Bradford Royal Infirmary), Leeds General Hospital and the Voluntary Broadcasting Service based in Otley (all in his spare time). He became very well known with guest spots on Radio 1, *Top of the Pops* (with Jimmy Savile), working for Peter Stringfellow's club Cinderella Rockafellas in Leeds, and as a compère at the Batley Variety Club.

One of his favourite ways to relax was visiting the Rock and Heifer in Thornton. One day he found he had bought the pub on a handshake with the landlord the previous evening (an ex-woolman's handshake is his promise). The business had been run down for some years, but John and his wife soon made it a popular and successful public house.

In the late 1980s John sold the thriving business, and while looking round for a new venture, he saw that the empty Midland Hotel, Bradford, was to be auctioned. He wasn't really interested but put in what he thought was a reasonable bid and soon found himself the new owner. The Midland, which had been closed for some time, needed a full modernisation, so with a small workforce (including himself and his wife) they refurbished the entire hotel. After many months of hard work and headaches the hotel reopened in 1993; and without John Pennington it would have joined the other Bradford icons that had been demolished over the years to make way for a road-widening scheme or a car park.

After several successful years, John was made an offer he could not refuse and sold the Midland. This left a void in his life. Along came the next venture, the Mecca on Manningham Lane. With his love of show business and a realisation that there was a need for more entertainment in the city, he developed Pennington's, which is now one of the leading venues in the north of England, where many top groups and artists appear. With hard work, a gift for enterprise and a business outlook given only to a chosen few, John has succeeded where many have failed.

He lives with his family at the sixteenth-century West Riddlesden Hall, Keighley, and is a very enthusiastic member and past president of the Bradford Chamber of Commerce.

Edward Petherbridge

Actor

Edward Petherbridge decided to become an actor in the gallery of the Bradford Alhambra in 1943 while watching Norman Evans in the pantomime *Humpty Dumpty*.

He was born on 3 August 1936 at the family home, 71 Pembroke Street, West Bowling. At St Stephen's Junior School off Manchester Road he was cast in his first play, *Barney Blue Eyes*. Later, while a pupil at Grange Grammar School, he decided to become a member of the Sedbergh Boys' Club in Bradford. It was with them, while taking part in a local drama festival, that he was spotted by the Bradford actor, producer and adjudicator, Walter Williams, who gave him the acting award. Not long afterwards he became a student at Esmé Church's Northern Theatre School, Bradford.

After early experiences in weekly rep – at one point rehearsing *Rookery Nook* by day and playing in Arthur Miller's *All My Sons* at night in Eastbourne, and similarly juggling Shakespeare and Agatha Christie at Hornchurch – he toured with Cicely Courtneidge, Jack Hulbert and Robertson Hare before playing in the classics at Regent's Park in 1963, and in Laurence Olivier's National Theatre at the Old Vic in 1964 where he stayed for six years.

As a founder member of the Actors' Company in 1972 (with Sir Ian McKellen) his many roles included Mirabel in *The Way of the World*, drawing on his early memories of variety at the Bradford Alhambra. As a member of the Royal Shakespeare Company he played Newman Noggs in *Nicholas Nickleby*, for which he won the London Theatre Critics' Award and a Tony nomination.

In 1984 he won an Olivier Award at the Duke of York's Theatre in London for his performance in Eugene O'Neill's *Strange Interlude*. The following year he returned to Broadway with the show and was again nominated for a Tony.

In 2002 he appeared with Jeffrey Archer in Archer's play *The Accused* on tour and at the Haymarket, London. Edward later performed his own one-man show at the West Yorkshire Playhouse, *Defending Jeffrey*.

His most famous television role has been Lord Peter Wimsey for the BBC and recently he has appeared as the toy-maker in the smash hit *Chitty Chitty Bang Bang* at the London Palladium. With numerous awards over many years, Edward is still in great demand and on a par with those other great Shakespearean actors Sir Donald Wolfit and Sir Henry Irving.

Duncan Preston

Actor

Duncan Preston discovered his love for acting when he attended the Bradford Civic Playhouse during the 1960s. He was born on 11 August 1946 at the family home, 120 Pullan Avenue, Eccleshill. He attended Wellington Road Primary and Junior Schools, and later Bradford Grammar.

Leaving school at sixteen, Duncan worked for his father in the haulage business and then in the Halifax Building Society in Bradford. He became interested in a local church stage group and later joined drama classes at the Bradford Playhouse, where he acted with distinction in numerous productions. In 1967 he won a place at RADA in London, where he spent two years, and was awarded two of the Academy's top awards, graduating with honours.

Duncan is well known for his roles in the TV sitcoms *Dinnerladies* and *Surgical Spirit*. His long-standing collaboration with Victoria Wood has seen him take on many characters in her *All Day Breakfast* and *Sketch Show Story*. He has appeared in two films written by Wood: *Pat and Margaret* and *Happy since I Met You*, both of which starred Julie Walters. He has also made regular appearances as Kevin the Teenager's dad in BBC1's *Harry Enfield and Chums*. His television appearances read like a guide to prime-time viewing: *The Professionals, All Creatures Great and Small, Bergerac, Heartbeat, Casualty, The Bill, Boon, Peak Practice, Coogan's Run, Midsomer Murders, Holby City, Merseybeat, The Royal* and *Born and Bred*.

His impressive range of theatre credits includes roles in Royal Shakespeare Company productions of *Romeo and Juliet, Pillar of the Community* and *A Midsummer Night's Dream*. His film credits include *Porridge, A Passage to India, Robin Hood, Scandalous, If Tomorrow Comes, Macbeth* and *Milk*.

Duncan is a frequent visitor to Bradford and has a great fondness for the district. He is also a keen supporter of the Bradford Bulls, rugby's world champions, and travels to watch them play at every opportunity. He says the Civic Playhouse gave him a purpose, enabled him to find something he could do and make a living out of it: 'If it was not for that place, I'd probably have ended up a lorry driver.'

For his contributions to acting Duncan was awarded a honorary doctorate in December 2000 by Bradford University.

J.B. Priestley OM

Author and Playwright

John Boynton Priestley – the 'Boynton' was a youthful affectation – is at the very heart of Bradford. The university library is the J.B. Priestley Library; the Bradford Playhouse is now the Priestley Centre for the Arts; his statue stands looking out over the city he loved so dearly – the city that awarded him its freedom; and the J.B. Priestley Society holds an annual Priestley Dinner at the Bradford Club.

Jack Priestley was born on 13 September 1894 at 34 Mannheim Road, off Toller Lane. The family moved to nearby 5 Saltburn Place ten years later (a blue plaque – high up – adorns the latter). Son of a schoolmaster, he worked as a junior clerk at Helm & Company, a shipping firm, in Swan Arcade, Market Street, before service in the infantry during the First World War. He was badly gassed in the trenches. He then went to Cambridge University, and after graduating, settled in London to become a writer, although some pieces had been accepted earlier in Bradford newspapers. He made his name as a journalist and a critic before his first big success, *The Good Companions* (1929), brought him household recognition – the description of a happy football crowd walking home after a match sticks in this author's mind.

Priestley's literary output was phenomenal, with a rapid succession of novels, plays and articles. Of his more than fifty plays, *An Inspector Calls* (a psychological mystery) and *When We Are Married* (a West Riding farce) are just two that are still regularly performed. His 'Time' plays, such as *Dangerous Corner, We Have Been Here Before* and *Time and the Conways*, are also regularly revived. *English Journey* and *Postscripts* are two of his better-known non-fiction works. The latter are the popular wartime broadcasts, in which Priestley's broad Yorkshire speech and down-to-earth delivery brought reassurance to the citizens of the country at a very nervous time. *Margin Released* contains accounts of his Bradford youth.

Priestley was a founder of the Campaign for Nuclear Disarmament and stood unsuccessfully as an independent MP at Oxford. He refused to be nominated for honours, but accepted the Order of Merit in 1977. He was awarded an honorary doctorate at the new University of Bradford in 1970 and the Freedom of the City of Bradford in 1973. He died on 14 August 1984, and is buried in the churchyard at Hubberholme in his beloved Yorkshire Dales.

This man of letters stood outside any movement or literary clique, but 'spoke for the common sense of the common man'.

Mike Priestley

Telegraph & Argus Journalist

Mike Priestley is probably Bradford's best-known journalist of modern times. He was born in Undercliffe, an area that gave Bradford many of its celebrities, and his column has a common touch to which local people can relate.

Born in a nursing home in Killinghall Road in January 1944, he moved to Great Horton with his mother, who rented a back-to-back house for the two of them in Halstead Place while his father was still in the army.

War over and the snowy winter of 1947 out of the way, the family moved to Wyke for a while. There Mike began his schooldays at the local primary school, but not for long. The family moved to Harehill Road in Thackley, to the north of Bradford, to their first 'bought' house. It was there that Mike grew up and found himself following in famous literary footsteps. He went first to Thackley Primary, where some years earlier John Braine of *Room at the Top* fame had been a pupil. And from there Mike passed his 11+ to go to Belle Vue Boys' Grammar School in Manningham Lane, where J.B. Priestley had been a pupil a few generations earlier.

He was not the most diligent pupil, and when he left school in 1962, aged eighteen, had managed to scrape through half a dozen O-level GCEs and a solitary A-level (English). This being the start of the '60s, he headed for London where he quickly found work as an editorial trainee on a trade magazine, *The Paint, Oil and Colour Journal*. 'It was all about resins and pigments and the like, and a bit boring', he admits. 'But the people were lovely and it gave me a start in this strange business of journalism.' Bradford pulled him back and he returned north at the end of the year to take up a post on the *Wool Record*, a magazine serving the wool trade and wool-textile industry.

Five years later he moved into the world of local newspapers as a sub-editor on the *Halifax Courier*, transferring after six months to a similar job with the Bradford's *Telegraph & Argus* at the end of 1968. He worked as a sub-editor by day and in the evenings covered the local pop-music scene for the newspaper. He soon moved into the features department and launched 'Priestley's Patch', the first of several columns he was to write among various other production and managerial duties. In the 1980s he stepped off the lower rungs of the management ladder to write full-time for the *T&A*, producing features on a wide range of subjects.

One of his finest coups, he reckons, was an impromptu interview with Paul McCartney at the BBC in London, although he believes his best work was a series of features he wrote after visiting Aberfan in the wake of the Valley Parade fire, to see how Bradford could learn from the way the Welsh village had coped with its own tragedy.

In the early 1980s he began to write 'North of Watford', a weekly opinion column in which, as he puts it, 'I'm privileged to be able to sound off about anything that takes my fancy or catches my eye.' It was 'North of Watford' that

three times won him the title of Columnist of the Year in the Yorkshire Press Awards. He was named Yorkshire Journalist of the Year in 1988.

He has also spent the last fourteen years writing a fortnightly walking column. 'I reckon I've covered over 2,000 miles on foot around this lovely county of ours in that time, in the line of duty', he says. 'And I hope I have encouraged a few people to buy a pair of boots and start walking themselves.'

Mike is married to Maureen, his childhood sweetheart, and they have a grown-up son and daughter. He still nurses an ambition to follow in the literary footsteps of Braine and Priestley and, as he puts it, 'produce a decent work of fiction'.

Bertram Priestman

Artist

Bertram Priestman broke away from his family's involvement in the wool industry to study art. He earned universal recognition as a first-rate artist and his paintings hang in galleries throughout the world.

Born in 1868, the son of a Bradford wool man and Quaker, he lived at Moorfield, Toller Lane, Heaton. He took to drawing as a child. The young artist began his education at Oliver's Mount, Scarborough, and the Friends' School, Bootham, York, after which he went on a tour of Italy with a sketchbook, a tour which also included trips to Egypt and Palestine. On his return he spent some months studying engineering at Bradford Technical College.

His real love was art and after a time at the Bradford College he gained a place at the Slade School in London. He was only twenty-two years old when the Royal Academy accepted two of his paintings, one of which was praised by critics as 'a modern Constable'. In 1891 he took a studio of his own in Chelsea and at once found his market, his paintings being purchased by well-known collectors. He married Grace Henwood in 1896, granddaughter of William Henwood, who had been the chief constructor of Chatham Dockyard. They lived in Chiswick at his residence and studio.

In the years before the First World War he painted on the Suffolk coast at Walberswick, and came under the influence of Wilson Steer. When war came he moved his wife and children to his native Yorkshire and lived at Box Tree Cottage, Starbottom, in Upper Wharfedale, where many of his famous landscapes were painted. His work at this period led to his election as an Associate of the Royal Academy.

Perhaps his rural scenes meant the most to him, notably the Wharfedale paintings *Evening Buckden, Haytime among the Hills, His Majesty's Mail, Kilnsey Crag* and the *The Becks of Beckermond*. His painting of Bradford, *Outskirts of a Northern City*, was described as 'a modern masterpiece' and was bought by the York Club, Toronto. With most of his paintings he kept close to the English landscape tradition of Constable and Turner, though he had earlier absorbed Dutch and French influences.

Bertram Priestman died at St Giles, Crowborough, Sussex, on 20 March 1951 aged eighty-three.

Michael Rennie

Actor

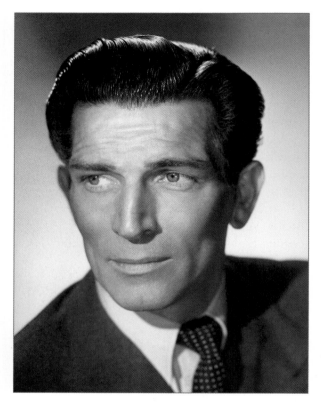

Michael Rennie was born in Bradford on 25 August 1909 in the area known as Brownroyd, Girlington, then moving to Norman Bank, Idle Road, before his family moved to Harrogate. After attending Oaklands Preparatory School, Harrogate, and the Leys School, Cambridge, he entered his father's business, W.M. Rennie & Co., worsted spinners at Stanningley. After trying his hand at worsted spinning, car salesmanship and steel rope manufacturing he decided to turn to the theatre, spending several seasons at York Repertory.

Rennie began to make a name for himself in films, albeit small parts, from 1936. In 1941 he secured a larger role in the successful film *Dangerous Moonlight*. Then came a break in his career when he served in the Second World War as a flying officer in the RAF. Rennie went to the United States to be an instructor in Georgia, but he was discharged (medically fit) from the RAF before the end of the war.

Once back in England he was soon making films again, including a specially written part in Rank's big 1945 film *Caesar and Cleopatra*, but then after the success of *The Wicked Lady* and *I'll Be Your Sweetheart* he signed a contract with Twentieth Century Fox. With Fox, Rennie's career truly began to blossom with major roles in the 1950s in *The Day the Earth Stood Still* (the sci-fi classic for which he is probably best remembered), *Les Miserables*, *The Robe* and many other films. Cinemagoers hailed Rennie as the young Yorkshireman who was, in appearance and style, similar to James Mason and Stewart Grainger.

In 1960 he went to live in Hollywood and became an American citizen. On television Rennie spent two years and 76 episodes portraying the suave soldier of fortune Harry Lime on the syndicated series *The Third Man*, and towards the end of the decade he appeared in the popular sci-fi series *The Invaders*.

In June 1971 while on a visit to his elderly mother in Harrogate, he was taken ill and died. He was buried in Harlow Hill Cemetery, Harrogate.

Tony Richardson

Director and Screen Writer

Tony Richardson rose from the head of Oxford University's dramatic society to the pinnacle of the British film industry during the early 1960s, scoring several theatrical successes as a director, notably *Look Back in Anger* by John Osborne.

Cecil Antonio Richardson was born on 5 June 1928 in Saltaire Road, Shipley. His early theatrical career was spent as a member of Bradford Civic Playhouse. He was associate director of the English Stage Company from 1956 to 1964. His first success was *Look Back in Anger*, followed by *The Entertainer*, both of which would later be filmed by Richardson's company, Woodfall Films. This was at a time when the new 'kitchen sink' dramas were brought to British cinema screens during the boom years of the 1960s.

Many up-and-coming young working-class actors made their debuts in such films as *Saturday Night and Sunday Morning*, *The Loneliness of the Long Distance Runner* and the film that brought him two Oscars in 1963, *Tom Jones*. Unfortunately, Richardson's 1968 reworking of *The Charge of the Light Brigade* was not a hit at the box office, and he did not repeat the success of his 1950s and '60s films.

The father of actresses Natasha and Joely, he died at the age of sixty-three in Los Angeles on 14 November 1991.

William Riley

Novelist

In his middle years William Riley became a prolific author with over thirty-five popular novels to his name. He was famous in his day, but is now, perhaps, largely forgotten. His best-known novel was *Windyridge* (1912). Set in the village of Hawksworth, it sold well over half a million copies.

William was born on 23 April 1866 at Bradford Moor. The Rileys were comfortably off – William's father was an ambitious mill manager in Bradford and was far-sighted enough to send his sons to Bradford Grammar School. William then joined his father's firm in Ivegate, but later, with his brother, founded a new firm of optical lantern-slide makers in the centre of Bradford.

Business and his work for the Methodist church were William's life until middle age. It was then that he wrote his first novel, *Windyridge*, but he had no thought of having it published. It was intended to entertain his wife and some of her friends; he read it to them chapter by chapter as he wrote it. In 1912, yielding to their persuasion, he sent the novel to Herbert Jenkins, publishers. Jenkins swooped on it – he thought it had been written by a woman, and in his acceptance of the novel addressed the author as 'Dear Miss Riley'. The early impact of *Windyridge* was staggering. By October it had been rushed through the press and Riley's name was made.

Such was the impression the book made on the public that hundreds of houses all over the country were named after that cottage in Hawksworth that William Riley described in the book. The charm of Riley's novels lay in their homely simplicity; there is faithful reproduction of the Yorkshire scene and of the life that people lived in humble abodes.

At the age of forty-five, William Riley started to live by his pen. His leisure was spent studying theology, tramping the Yorkshire Dales and preaching on Sundays (he had been a Methodist lay preacher since 1886).

In 1919, due to his wife's ill health he moved to Silverdale near Morecambe, where he bought a house – and naturally called it Windyridge. While there he wrote many books about the Yorkshire Dales.

Still writing well into his nineties, but with failing health, he died at St Anne's, Morecambe, on 4 June 1961 at ninety-five.

David Roper

Actor

David Roper shot to fame in the 1970s in the Granada sitcom *The Cuckoo Waltz*, but it was his twice-weekly appearances in *EastEnders* that made him a household name for his role as Geoff Barnes, the middle-aged tutor who fell in love with Michelle Fowler.

He was born on 20 June 1944 at St Luke's Hospital. (Fifty-eight years later he was back in that same delivery room filming an episode of *The Royal* – the sister programme to *Heartbeat*.) The family lived in Midland Road, Manningham, and he attended the local junior school. Later, on a free scholarship, he went to Bradford Grammar School.

After leaving school David studied for six years to be an accountant, working at Armitage & Norton and Dickinson & Keighley Accountants, both in Bradford. However, on the morning of 24 April 1967 he awoke, stared at the bedroom ceiling and thought: 'I want to be an actor.' Nothing in his life justified, let alone supported, such a drastic change of ambition. That day he enrolled in the Green Room classes at the Bradford Playhouse.

David quickly won a place at the Bristol Old Vic Theatre School. He then spent a year with the Bristol Old Vic itself as an assistant stage manager and actor. Now, with experience, he became a member of the Manchester Library Theatre Company. A period at the Northcott Theatre, Exeter, followed.

At this point he decided he should be in television, and was soon back in Manchester and playing the part of the copper who arrested Eddie Yates in *Coronation Street*. He then played a policeman again in two other Granada productions, *My Brother's Keeper* and *Crown Court*. Other TV series included *Churchill's People* and *Country Tales*.

All this experience now led him to his most famous role in *The Cuckoo Waltz* playing a flat-broke local newspaper reporter with a young wife (Diane Keen) and a rich lodger (Lewis Collins). The programme attracted 17 million viewers at its peak between 1975 and 1980. *The Cuckoo Waltz*'s success earned him a sitcom of his own, *Leave It to Charlie*. After that show ended he did many commercial tours.

In the 1980s his television career revived. He played a policeman once more in Michael Elphick's series *Harry*. He then appeared on almost every other show on television playing policemen. Finally, *EastEnders* came: David came to Albert Square as the college lecturer Geoff.

David is one of the few actors who have worked on *EastEnders* and *Coronation Street*, and still crops up on our screens regularly. In between his television roles he has returned to the theatre, recently on a UK tour with a prestigious production of J.B. Priestley's *An Inspector Calls*, including a performance at the Alhambra Theatre in his home town of Bradford.

Sir William Rothenstein

Artist

'Nothing would please me more than to return to Bradford and live among my people and find my inspiration in the surrounding county. The bare bald hills and moors, the mills even, have a strange fascination for me, and I would give much to spend my life amid the scenes of my earlier days.'

William Rothenstein was born at 4 Spring Bank, Manningham Lane, on 29 January 1872, to a Jewish family from Hamelin, Germany. His father Moritz, a wool merchant, became a Unitarian, but continued to support the Jewish community in Bradford. William's education began at one of the local preparatory schools in Manningham and continued at Bradford Grammar School.

On leaving the school at the age of sixteen he enrolled at the Slade School of Art in London. After working under Alphonse Legros he moved to Paris where he associated with Henri de Toulouse-Lautrec and Camille Pissarro. Aged 19 he held his first exhibition, and began his unique series of portrait drawings which ultimately included Oscar Wilde, Rudyard Kipling, T.E. Lawrence and King Edward VIII. In 1893 he was closely associated with Augustus John, Walter Sickert, Wilson Steer and his brother-in-law, Sir William Orpen, in the New English Art Club, and he continued to be a regular contributor to the club's exhibitions.

On the outbreak of the First World War his German name and accent made him unpopular in the Gloucestershire village where he lived. A patriotic Englishman, he quickly accepted the offer of Charles Masterman, the head of the government's War Propaganda Bureau, to become an official war artist. He visited the Somme front in December 1917. He stayed with the British Fifth Army in 1918 and during the German spring offensive he served as an unofficial medical orderly. His pictures *Ypres Salient* and *Talbot House, Ypres* were exhibited in May 1918.

In 1920 Rothenstein became principal of the Royal College of Art, a post he held until 1935. He had been knighted in 1931 and in 1934 was given an honorary doctorate by Oxford University. Sheffield University also conferred an MA degree on him.

Although he was sixty-seven when the Second World War began, he again became a war artist, this time with the Royal Air Force. In this capacity he made over 200 portraits of members of all ranks of the RAF whom he visited at their stations.

Despite living away from Bradford, Rothenstein frequently returned to his parents' home at 6 Walmer Villas, Manningham, and had many artistic contacts with Bradford, sending a number of his paintings to Cartwright Memorial Hall.

Sir William Rothenstein died on 14 February 1945 at his home at Far Oakridge, Stroud, Gloucestershire, aged seventy-three.

Simon Rouse

Actor

While his name may not be instantly recognisable, his face certainly is to millions of viewers who watch the weekly police drama *The Bill*, in which he plays the no-nonsense Detective Chief Inspector Jack Meadows.

Simon was born in St Luke's Hospital, Bradford, in 1951 when the family were living on the Haworth Road estate. In 1955 they moved to Jesmond Avenue. He attended St Barnabas's Junior School, Heaton, and then Lorne Street School, where his father was a teacher, for his last year.

Simon's childhood days hold many happy memories, playing around the Lister's Mill area, going on raids to pinch other streets' accumulation of wood leading up to bonfire night, and being chased by the infamous Beamsley Road Gang. Like many others who played around the area at that time he believed the famous story that a horse and cart could be driven round the top of Lister's mill chimney because it was so large!

He joined the Bradford Cathedral Choir where he enjoyed the music, dressing up and all the ceremony it entailed. When he was ten the family moved to 8 Haslingden Drive, off Toller Lane. A year later he passed his 11+. Moving to Belle Vue Grammar School, he joined the scouts and enjoyed their camping holidays in the Dales.

About this time he discovered acting and from then on nothing else mattered. He joined the school drama society and later the Bradford-based Group Theatre in Westgate. After leaving school he worked at weekends at Morrison's, Girlington, alongside Tony McHale, also a member of the Group Theatre (now a successful TV writer). Simon also had another job in Kirkgate Market. The new Bradford Library was a meeting place meant for rehearsing, but he spent more time in the café 'chatting'. Partying was done at the Elmer discotheque in Shipley, the university dances, or the Interlingual Club which was in a cellar off Manningham Lane full of au pair girls – he 'thought it was fantastic!'

In 1968 he spent five weeks in London with the National Youth Theatre and won a place at the Rose Bruford College in Sidcup. Just before he graduated he was offered a major role in the film *The Ragman's Daughter*, based on Alan Sillitoe's story of star-crossed lovers from opposite sides of the track. Simon, who played the lead, saw the film in 1972 at the ABC cinema on Broadway, Bradford.

He has played at the Alhambra Theatre with the Royal Court production of *The Changing Room* and also his own production of *Ghosts*. He has worked with the Royal Shakespeare Company and starred in many London stage productions. TV appearances include *The Professionals* (1977), *Dr Who* (1982), *Robin of Sherwood* (1984), *EastEnders* (1984), *Bread* (1986) and *Boon* (1987). Then he landed the part of the tough-talking DCI Meadows of Sun Hill, a role which has changed his life and turned him into a star at home and abroad. He has said, 'Bradford will always be dear to my heart.'

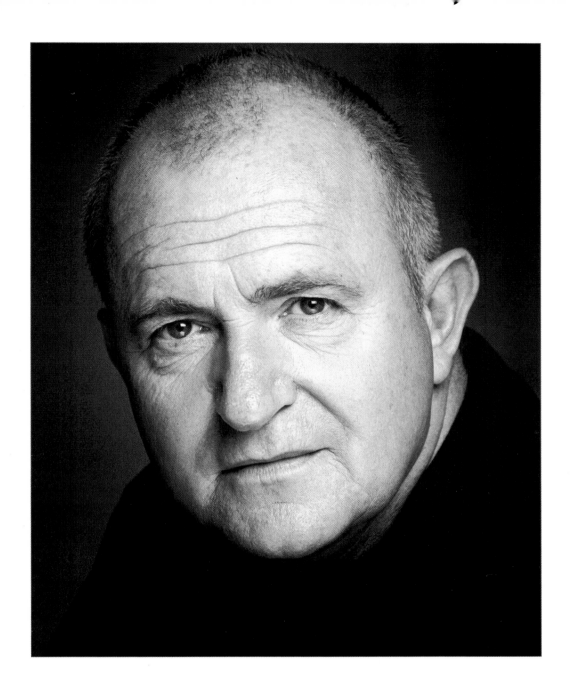

Sir Titus Salt

Wool Baron

In the early 1800s Bradford was about to become the centre of the worsted trade in England, and was entering a boom period that was to last almost 150 years. Steam mills had arrived, power-looms and combing-machines were coming into use, labour troubles and Luddite riots were settling down, the Victorian era, glossy, lush and complacent was close at hand. Bradford was a kind of Klondyke to which the enterprising, such as Titus Salt, were drawn.

Titus was born on 20 September 1803 in Morley, where his father worked as a dry salter and wool merchant. He sent Titus to Heath Grammar School. The family later moved to Crofton, Wakefield, to take up farming. When this failed they moved to Bradford.

Salt senior set up as a wool-stapler in a small way, while Titus, to gain further experience, went for two years to Rouse & Son, worsted spinners. Rejoining his father in 1824, he attended wool sales in London and Liverpool, travelling to buy wool from farmers in Norfolk and Lincolnshire, and sold wool to many firms in the West Riding towns. The firm, Daniel Salt & Son, prospered and became one of the most important textiles companies in Bradford.

When Daniel Salt retired in 1833, Titus took over the running of the company, which now owned five textile mills in Bradford. In 1848 he became Lord Mayor of Bradford, and tried hard to persuade the council to pass a by-law that would force all factory owners in the town to use the new smoke burners that reduced pollution. The other factory owners in Bradford were opposed to the idea, and refused to accept that the smoke produced by their factories was damaging people's health.

When he realised the council was unwilling to take action, he decided to move from Bradford and announced his plans to build a new industrial community called Saltaire in nearby countryside on the banks of the River Aire. The mill opened on Salt's fiftieth birthday, 20 September 1853. It was the largest and most modern in Europe, and to ensure that the neighbourhood did not suffer from polluted air, the mill chimney was fitted with Rodda smoke burners. At its peak fourteen boilers supplied steam for four beam engines which powered 1,200 looms that were capable of producing 30,000 yards of cloth per day.

At first Salt's 3,500 workers travelled to Saltaire from the Bradford districts. During the next few years, however, 850 houses were built for his workforce. When completed, Saltaire had its own park, church, school, hospital, library, and a whole range of different shops. The houses in Saltaire were far superior to those available in any other industrial town. Fresh water was piped into each home, gas was laid on to provide lighting and heating, and every family in Saltaire had its own outside lavatory. To encourage people to keep themselves clean he arranged for public baths and wash-houses to be built. There were no public houses in the village; a club and institute were erected to cater for the moral and physical welfare of the community.

In 1859 Salt became Liberal Member of Parliament for Bradford, but resigned in 1861 due to ill-health.

He distributed his wealth in magnificent profusion, with gifts for the erection of public buildings and the founding of scholarships at the Bradford Grammar School. He gave thousands of pounds to orphanages, hospitals, churches and charities of all kinds. He gave a lifeboat to Stornaway and contributed to the cost of the Royal Albert Hall. In 1869 he accepted a baronetcy.

On his seventieth birthday, by now a patriarchal figure, he entertained over 4,000 of his workers at his home, Crow Nest, at Lightcliffe near Brighouse. It was there on 29 December 1876 that he died aged seventy-three. Many dignitaries and thousands of ordinary working-class people attended the funeral. The route the cortège took from Brighouse to Saltaire passed through the centre of Bradford, past the Town Hall where his imposing statue was draped in black, on through to Shipley and Saltaire where he was laid to rest in the large family mausoleum opposite his mill.

Leslie Sands

Actor

Leslie Sands was born on 19 May 1921 in a back-to-back house at 11 Grant Street. Both his mother and father, Alice and Albert, were hands at the local mill and attended Holy Trinity Church, Leeds Road, where they were married in 1919. His father was a survivor of the 16th Battalion West Yorkshire Regiment, one of the renowned 'Bradford Pals'.

Leslie first attended Barkerend Infants School, then Hanson Junior and High School, where he took part in theatrical drama, appearing in plays at St Clement's Church. In 1937 he left school to work for Sternol Oil in Manningham Lane, but realised he had made a mistake and returned to school in 1938 to take the Higher School Certificate. He gained a place at Leeds University where his acting and studying marched hand in hand. During one vacation he auditioned at a professional theatre in Leeds and was accepted as a paid actor, thus acquiring valuable experience which was to serve him well, and give him entry to Equity.

When war came he joined the RAF and was a radar mechanic, progressing to sergeant instructor. During the war he was at Cranwell in Lincolnshire where he met Peter Sallis. Together they set up the Little Theatre on the base. It is some measure of the value of his effort that the theatre is still in existence.

After the war he was able to claim with justice that he had experience as a professional actor, and could plunge straight back into the theatre. His first stage appearance in London was in 1946, taking a small part in a production of *Antony and Cleopatra* with Godfrey Tearle and Dame Edith Evans. In this and other parts he soon established himself as the archetypal hard-bitten man of the Dales. It was in the BBC series *Cluff* that the tweed hat, walking stick and dog made Sands' country policeman a TV legend in 1964 and 1965.

He was equally at home in comedy, appearing in *Cilla's Comedy Six*, *Man About the House*, and many cameo parts in such shows as *The Planemakers*, *Z Cars*, *Blackadder*, *The Two Ronnies* and *The Fall and Rise of Reginald Perrin*. He played many supporting roles in a number of films including Disney's *Escape from the Dark*, *The Ragman's Daughter* and *The Deadly Affair*.

He wrote twenty stage plays, more than seventy television scripts, three novels and an interesting autobiography, *Tuppence for the Rainbow*. He was a member of the Royal Shakespeare Company and a National Theatre player. Leslie Sands was a true Bradfordian, he never forgot his roots and made many visits to the city.

He died at Chepstow, Monmouthshire, on 9 May 2001 aged seventy-nine.

Len Shackleton

Bradford and England Footballer

Len Shackleton was an outstanding postwar footballer, although he only appeared for England on five occasions – a small number of caps for such a skilful player.

Born in Bradford on 22 May 1922, he was brought up in Horton Bank Top, and educated at Carlton High School. At a young age he was already an impressive footballer. He became Bradford's first player to appear for England Schools and won three caps against Wales and Scotland.

When he was sixteen Leonard Francis Shackleton of 38 Soaper Lane left Bradford to join Arsenal Football Club as an amateur player, and was given a job in the office while receiving the necessary coaching and training to become a professional. It was all to no avail because Arsenal manager George Allison decided that he was too small to make the grade and sent him back to Yorkshire – their loss.

Back in his home city he made his mark with Bradford Park Avenue aged seventeen. When war broke out he was working in an aircraft factory, later as a Bevin Boy, but still continued playing for Bradford Park Avenue, scoring 160 goals during the wartime seasons. In 1945 he also won an English cap in the Victory International against Scotland.

Shackleton rapidly emerged as one of the most gifted inside forwards in the country, having spent six seasons at Park Avenue before joining Newcastle United in 1946 for £13,000. On his debut he scored 6 goals against Newport County in a 13–0 victory at St James's Park. But after only 18 months he joined Sunderland for £20,500, and spent the rest of his playing career at Roker Park. With Sunderland, Shackleton scored 98 league goals in 320 games for the Wearsiders. In all competitions he made a total of 348 appearances for the club and scored 101 times. The club also reached the FA Cup semi-finals and narrowly missed out on championship success. He won his five international caps between 1945 and 1954.

Perhaps his most famous appearance was when England defeated the world champions West Germany in 1954, when he scored in the 3–1 defeat. An ankle injury drew his career to a close, and in 1957 he became a journalist with the *Sunday People* and *Daily Express*.

At the peak of his career, when the football league financial constraints had a minimum wage, he was regularly watched by crowds of more than 50,000 people, all for £17 per week.

Len later retired to a flat overlooking Grange-over-Sands, but always retained his roots in Bradford, remembering how fierce the rivalry was between City and Park Avenue. After a short illness he died in November 2000 aged seventy-eight.

Ernest Leopold Sichel

Artist

Ernest Leopold Sichel was a man of many talents – portrait and landscape painter, artist in black and white, as well as a renowned sculptor. He was universally known and admired for the exceptional technical quality of his paintings.

He was born on 27 June 1862 in Ashfield, Great Horton. His father, a wool merchant, was a cultivated man, like many German immigrants, and encouraged his youngest son's artistic career. Ernest attended Bradford Grammar School and was a close friend of Frederick Delius who was a fellow scholar and whose home was opposite the Sichel house in Claremont off Great Horton Road.

Ernest's ability in art manifested itself early in life, and at fourteen he was taking private lessons from John Sowden, the well-known painter of Bradford characters. When he left school, with an encouraging verdict from Sir John Millais on a watercolour drawing of a bird subject, he proceeded to the Slade School of Art in London under Alphonse Legros, and later J.M. Swan, the animal painter who became his close friend as they had adjoining studios.

On leaving the Slade he occupied a studio in Euston Road, London, with his friend John Swan. With Swan he journeyed to Paris, among other reasons to study mural paintings of Pierre Puvis de Chavannes, who is considered to have influenced Sichel's work. Returning to Bradford in the 1880s he began to paint portraits among which those of the eminent local medical men, Dr Bell and Dr Bronner, and of Jacob Behrens, gave early proof of his great technical ability.

Oils, watercolours and pastels were not his only media. He also designed ecclesiastical embroidery, and bronze and silverwork. Foremost among his admirers was Sir William Rothenstein who wrote warmly of Sichel in his first volume of memoirs. While in Bradford he continued to exhibit at the Royal Academy, the New English Watercolour Club and the Pastel Society. Retrospective exhibitions of his work were held in Leeds in 1932, and at Cartwright Hall, Bradford, in 1973, several examples of his best work being in the permanent collection there, notably *Sir Jacob Behrens*, *Funeral of a Child in the Highlands* and *A Gaul* (bronze statuette).

He did beautiful work as a sculptor; Bradford Grammar School has an example of his skill in the bronzework of the War Memorial.

Over the years in his native city Sichel exercised his various talents in work of many kinds. He was a sensitive, infinitely modest man who always seemed to have a low opinion of his own attainments as if he feared the world. He was content to stay in Bradford and give his best to local people. Perhaps if he had stayed in London for fifty years his name might have been upon the lips of most of the art world of the twenty-first century.

Ernest Sichel, who was a bachelor, died on 21 March 1941 at 2 Claremont, where he spent most of his life after those London years.

Jonathan Silver
Salt's Mill Entrepreneur

Jonathan Silver, a man of outstanding ability, was one of those rare people who affected the future of an uncountable number of others. Through his entrepreneurial enterprises he left a permanent mark on Saltaire.

He was born in Bradford in 1949 at Clifton Villas, Manningham, where his grandmother ran a boarding house. Jonathan attended Bradford Junior Grammar School, then the Senior Grammar School on Keighley Road. He disliked school and was always bottom of the class, but did manage to leave with sufficient GCEs to take a degree in fine arts a few years later.

During his school years he spent his lunch breaks at the local auction rooms gaining knowledge of antiques and their values. Aged fifteen he started buying and selling furniture at the auction rooms in Bradford, developing this and other little businesses, which brought him early financial satisfaction.

On leaving school he started several businesses in Manchester – furniture, art prints and men's clothing. He was so successful in the latter that by 1980 he had thirteen clothing shops spread around the country with a £1 million turnover.

One of Jonathan's cloth suppliers was Ernest Hall, the textile magnate. Together they bought Dean Clough Mill in Halifax, planning to use the massive mill space to exhibit paintings and events. Despite their friendship they were incompatible as business partners. After a year, Jonathan sold his shares to Ernest.

After travelling round the world with his wife and family for three years, he looked around for a new enterprise. In 1987 he bought the semi-derelict Salt's Mill. His days were long, organising architectural restructuring to build and develop public spaces at the mill. One of his many successes is the permanent space to exhibit art work in the 1853 Galleries, which includes works by his long-time friend David Hockney. Bringing business to the building was another of Jonathan's visions, and in 1990 Pace Micro Technology moved into Salt's Mill. In 1995 Filtronic Comtek's factory was opened in the grounds of Salt's Mill and this contributed to the mill's winning the Civic Trust Centre Vision Award. In the same year Saltaire and Salt's Mill won the Europa Nostra Award for conservation-led regeneration, Europe's highest accolade.

Jonathan Silver did more to regenerate Bradford's ailing buildings than anyone else. The truth can be seen in his legacy. Previously beautiful buildings had been left empty to be vandalised and finally demolished, which is surely what would have happened at Salt's Mill if he had not been in the right place at the right time.

Sadly, after a long illness he died at his home on 25 September 1997 aged forty-seven.

Guy Bracewell Smith
Lord Mayor of London

Guy Bracewell Smith has often been compared with Dick Whittington, and there is an element of the fairy tale in the rise of the pupil-teacher from Ingrow who became Lord Mayor of London.

Born on 1 January 1884 in Wesley Place, Keighley, which overlooked the Worth Valley Railway, he was educated at Leeds University, graduating with a BSc before moving to London in 1907. In 1909 he married Edith Whitaker, a girl from Bingley. Having chosen a career he settled as a science teacher, but after service in the Royal Engineers in the First World War he dramatically changed direction.

It would be almost impossible to give details of the financial stratagems with which he built his empire of prestigious London properties including the Park Lane Hotel and the Café Royal in Regent Street. He launched his business career with only £2,000, raised a loan of £40,000, and bought the Shaftesbury Hotel in London.

He combined business with public service, joining the London County Council in 1923 and was elected Mayor of Holborn 1931–2. In 1932 and 1945 he was MP for Dulwich, knighted in 1945, elected Lord Mayor of London in 1946–7 and was made a baronet in 1947.

He lived in Park Lane, and became Chairman of Wembley Stadium in 1957 and Arsenal Football Club from 1949–1961. Never forgetting his roots, he bought Cliffe Castle and its grounds in 1949 and presented it to his home town of Keighley, along with large sums of money for its restoration. Henceforth Keighley had a Museum and Art Gallery to be proud of. In 1957 he was made an Honorary Freeman of the Borough of Keighley.

Sir Guy Bracewell Smith died on 12 January 1966 aged eighty-one.

Harvey Smith

International Show Jumper

Harvey Smith, arguably the most famous show jumper of all time, is an equal of those two other no-nonsense sporting Yorkshire men, Fred Truman and Brian Close.

Born on 29 December 1938 in Gilstead, he was educated at Eldwick Primary and Bingley Secondary Modern schools. From an early age he had always been interested in horses, in particular equestrian sport, achieving his first show jumping success on a Gilstead milk cart pony. Since then he has won many of show jumping's top prizes and greatest honours. He rode such fine horses as Harvester, O'Malley and Madison Time, and represented Great Britain at the 1968 and 1972 Olympic Games before turning professional.

Among his many talents he has been a professional wrestler, television commentator, singer and comedian. Perhaps not all were successful, but with true Yorkshire grit he gave it a go.

Harvey's life has not been without controversy and he has never been afraid to air his forthright views. At Hickstead in 1971 he caused a national outcry when he allegedly gave the 'V' sign to the course owner after winning the British Show Jumping Derby. Subsequently the phrase 'doing a Harvey Smith' crept into the English language.

Harvey still lives near where he was born at Craiglands Farm on the edge of Ilkley Moor with his wife Sue, one of the top twenty National Hunt racehorse trainers in Britain. His two sons Robert and Stephen also became top show jumpers.

Philip Snowden

Politician

One of the founders of the British Labour Party, Philip Snowden worked as an early campaigner with Keir Hardie, also as a Labour Member of Parliament and as Chancellor of the Exchequer in two Labour governments.

He was born on 18 July 1864 at the wool weaving village of Cowling, on the moors about seven miles from Keighley. He was raised in a hamlet on the edge of Cowling called Ickornshaw (a community of about 100 cottages), educated at a private school in Cowling and also received education from the Wesleyan Sunday School. Philip did well at school and at the age of fifteen started work as a clerk in an insurance office. It was later, because of a cycling accident which crippled him for life, that he took up politics.

He joined the Keighley Liberal Club, but became converted to the new Independent Labour Party where he soon gained a reputation as a fine orator and drew large crowds. It was said that only Keir Hardie was his equal as a platform speaker.

In 1899 Snowden was elected to the Keighley Town Council and School Board. He also served as editor of the local socialist newspaper. He made several attempts to enter the House of Commons, but was defeated at Blackburn in the 1900 general election and at a by-election in Wakefield in 1902. He finally succeeded in the 1906 general election when he was elected Labour MP for Blackburn. He was twice National Chairman of the Labour Party.

Snowden belonged to the pacifist minority of the socialist group during the First World War. He served in the House of Commons from 1906 to 1918, and like other anti-war Labour MPs he was defeated in the 1918 general election. However, he was elected to represent Colne Valley in the 1922 general election. As an acknowledged specialist in finance, he became Chancellor of the Exchequer in the first-ever Labour government, formed in 1923 by Ramsay MacDonald. He held this position in the second Labour government from 1929 to 1931.

He remained Chancellor in the National Government of 1931, but did not stand in the 1931 general election. Instead he accepted the title that enabled him to sit in the House of Lords, Viscount Snowden of Ickornshaw. He served as Lord Privy Seal 1931–2 but resigned when free trade was abandoned.

During the last few years he was a sick man and died at his home in Telford on 15 May 1937. He was cremated at Woking and his ashes were scattered on the open moor near Ickornshaw where he played as a child.

Marie Studholme

Gaiety Girl and Actress

Marie Studholme was the most photographed woman of the stage in the 1890s and early 1900s, and is best remembered as one of the most popular postcard beauties of her day, rivalled only by the Dare Sisters and Gabrielle Ray. Her pictures sold in their thousands.

Caroline Marie Studholme Lupton was born on 10 September 1875 in Hall Lane, Eccleshill, but was brought up in Baildon. She was the daughter of a middle-class family – her father Joseph Studholme Lupton was an auctioneer who had offices in Bradford. Educated at a preparatory school before moving to Salt's School she was noted for her sweet nature and her love of other children and animals. On leaving school she worked for a time in her father's business, but after small parts in amateur dramatics, with her father's consent she made her way to London, where she stayed with family friends.

So began her career in 1892 at the Criterion Theatre, London, under Charles Wyndham's management. She was afterwards engaged by George Edwardes for musical comedy in which she continued to play small parts in many West End productions.

At Daly's, London, she understudied Letty Lind in *An Artist's Model* (1895). In 1897 she made her first visit to the United States with Edwardes' number one company before returning to England, where she became increasingly popular in leading roles in London and on tour. During this time she had married an actor called Gilbert Porteus, but was divorced soon afterwards.

It is not widely known that Marie was one of the few women in Britain who studied jujitsu under the world-renowned Yukio Tani in 1907, and became quite an exponent of the art. Her career could be described as having been steady rather than exciting; she appeared before the public touring the United Kingdom and United States between the mid-1890s and 1915. The impression was that her presence on stage was charming rather than striking.

In 1908 she secretly married Giles Borrett who was not an actor, but to be near her he managed to appear as a member of the chorus in more than one of her shows. She had no children of her own, but later adopted two.

She was lady of very great personal attraction and for a number of years the most extensively photographed woman on stage in the country, from which it is said she made a fortune.

Marie Studholme died in London in 1930.

Mollie Sugden

Actress and Comedienne

Mollie Sugden is most famous for playing purple-haired Mrs Slocombe in *Are You Being Served?* but she has had a long and varied career on British TV screens.

Born in Thwaites Brow, Keighley, on 21 July 1922, she was three when the family moved to Braithwaite, where she attended Laycock Village School. The family then moved to Molsis Road, Keighley, and Mollie attended Keighley Girls' Grammar School.

During the Second World War Mollie worked at Royal Ordnance Factory in Steeton. After the war she went to London to train at the Guildhall School of Music and Dance where she became licentiate. Many years later she became a Member of the Guildhall School of Music.

Her first professional engagement was in Accrington, in weekly repertoire, where she remained for twelve weeks, then more weekly rep at the Oldham Coliseum. In all, she did eight years in weekly rep before joining Thora Hird in *Saturday Night at the Crown* by Walter Greenwood, which was her first summer season in Blackpool. She was to spent five summer seasons at Blackpool, as well as seasons in Eastbourne, Jersey, Bournemouth, and many tours with various plays.

Television followed, making her debut with Tyne Tees' *Under New Management* directed by David Croft. Then followed *Hugh and I* with Hugh Lloyd and Terry Scott, *Just Jimmy*, with Jimmy Clitheroe, *The Liver Birds*; *Son of the Bride*, *That's My Boy*, and *My Husband and I*, the last two with Yorkshire Television.

All this was to pale beside the legend she would create in the sitcom *Are You Being Served?*, which ran from 1972 to 1983, and was brought back in the 1992 sequel series *Grace and Favour*. Both are still shown worldwide, especially in America, where they are still very popular and Mrs Slocombe is quite a star.

Comedy is not her only craft; her drama credits include *Maggie* in 1964, the 1970 production of *The Six Wives of Henry VIII*, and Mrs Goddard in the 1972 mini-series *Emma*.

Apart from the occasional interview Mollie is now content to sit back and enjoy retirement; her tremendous contributions and memorable characters guarantee her a place in the hearts of British comedy fans forever.

Halliwell Sutcliffe

Novelist

Perhaps no author was ever so steeped in the lore and legend of Airedale and Wharfedale than Halliwell Sutcliffe, the Bradford-born author of more than forty romantic novels.

Born at a relative's house in Thackley on 25 April 1870, he was the son of John Sutcliffe of Oxenhope, who from 1873 to 1901 was the headmaster of Bingley Grammar School. At that time the family lived in Haworth, but when Halliwell was three they moved into the eighteenth-century School House, which stands behind Bingley Parish Church. Halliwell attended his father's school. He spent his formative years at the foot of the 'Bonniest highway in the Dales', the road to Harden and from there to the moors.

He won a scholarship to King's College, Cambridge, and in 1893 gained an MA degree with honours in mathematics. Nurturing from boyhood an ambition to write, after university he went to London and became a journalist. His first novel, *The Eleventh Commandment*, was published in 1895, in which Saxilton is a thinly disguised Bingley. His career as a novelist had begun.

For the background to his novels he drew heavily on the brooding landscapes of his infancy. Most of the novels are historical romances set in the Yorkshire Dales. Each place visited in his many books was brought alive by his acute sensitivity to local atmosphere, made real by his profound knowledge of local history. Significantly, his time in the metropolis is not referred to in any of his novels, and he longed to return to the green acres of which, while he was away, he wrote so poignantly.

After marriage in 1904, he brought his wife to live in the Manor House at Embsay, and then moved to a sixteenth-century grange in Linton which had once belonged to the White Friars.

In the next twenty-six years he wrote more than thirty novels, undoubtedly some of his best work, and it was at Linton in January 1932 that he died aged sixty-one.

Robert Lowry Turner
Pioneer in the Treatment of Cancer

'In the Royal Infirmary I found wards full of women suffering from cancer of the breast. They were basically awaiting death in the majority of cases. In those days there was no treatment beyond surgery and radio-therapy.' Robert Turner, author of these words, was born in Northern Ireland in 1923. He graduated from Queen's University, Belfast.

In 1956 Robert Turner was appointed as Consultant Pathologist at the Royal Infirmary, Bradford, where chemotherapy was confined to treating leukaemia only. With the collaboration with the well-known Bradford surgeon, George Whyte-Watson, he developed the drugs to treat cancer, particularly breast cancer. As a result, there was a dramatic increase in the survival rate of women suffering from this disease.

He had taken his inspiration from Dr J.F. Wilkinson under whom he worked as a research fellow at the Department of Haematology in Manchester in the mid-1950s. Dr Wilkinson had led the field in cancer research with the use of nitrogen mustard, a substance which had been used to lethal effect during the First World War as mustard gas.

In Bradford Professor Turner and Mr Whyte-Watson examined the effects on treating patients before, during and after surgery with injections of a mustard gas-derived chemical and the male sex hormone. When the team published their results in the *British Medical Journal* in 1959, there was consternation in the conservative medical profession, which objected most to the idea of a surgeon dabbling in medicine and a pathologist messing about with living patients!

To help build on this beginning a special Clinical Oncology Unit was created at Bradford University to push forward cancer research, and Professor Turner was appointed its first director. Thanks to him and his surgeon colleague, Bradford's War on Cancer Fund was set up in the 1970s to fund the unit entirely by voluntary donations.

He retired from the Royal Infirmary in 1981, but continued as Director of the University Unit until his retirement in 1988. Even in retirement he continued to treat patients at the Yorkshire Clinic at Cottingley and pressed on with his research at his laboratory in Oxenhope near Keighley.

In the 1980s Professor Turner discovered he had cancer, the very condition that he had devoted his life to combating. He died in December 1990 at the Yorkshire Clinic, aged sixty-seven.

There is a memorial plaque in Bradford Cathedral to commemorate Professor Turner's life.

Stephanie Turner

Actress

Stephanie Turner was born in Eccleshill in 1944, just before D-Day. Her father was in the army awaiting embarkation for the Normandy landings. Her mother's family had lived in Eccleshill for generations.

Aged three she went to Hutton School, but when the family moved to Bradford Moor in 1950, she went to Thornbury Infants and Junior School. There she was part of the 'Postwar Bulge', being one of fifty-two in her class. She passed her 11+ and went to Hanson Girls' Grammar School. Now one of a class of twenty-six, she loved this school, did well, and in 1966 went to the University of Manchester where she read for a degree in drama.

She had decided she wanted to be an actress when she was ten, a decision almost certainly based on the annual outing to the pantomime at the Alhambra. She had been to children's classes at the Civic Playhouse and later, as a teenager, went to the Prince's Theatre whenever funds allowed. At seventeen she joined a group of young people and formed a theatre club called Group Theatre with premises in Westgate.

Her first professional theatre job after graduating from Manchester University was in a children's theatre company, followed by her first rep, which was at the newly opened Swan Theatre in Worcester. Just before graduating she had met Alan Ayckbourn, who at that time was working as a radio producer for the BBC in Leeds, and Stephanie began what was to be a long and fruitful working relationship with him, first in radio and then in the theatre.

Over the years she has played leading roles in most of the major repertory companies including her favourite roles, Terry, in the original production of *How the Other Half Loves* by Ayckbourn, Blanche in *A Streetcar named Desire* by Tennessee Williams and the title roles in Tom Stoppard's *Rose* and *Hapgood*. In the West End her first part was a lead in Colin Welland's *Say Goodnight to Grandma* in 1973.

She has made countless television appearances from *Coronation Street*, *Z Cars* and *The Sweeney* in the early days, through to *A Touch of Frost*, *Life with the Braithwaites*, *Emmerdale*, *Boon*, *The Bill* and *Casualty*. She has also appeared in many single plays and films for TV including an award-winning production of *An Ideal Husband*, in which she played Mrs Erlynne.

She is, however, probably best known for starring as Inspector Jean Darblay in the police series *Juliet Bravo*, which she played for three series. For this she won the Variety Club of Great Britain award for BBC Personality of the Year.

Timothy West CBE
Actor and Director

Timothy West is among Britain's most revered and accomplished actors, a master at playing authoritative figures.

He was born on 20 October 1934 at a nursing home on Manningham Lane, Bradford. His parents were stage and radio stars Lockwood West and Olive Carleton-Crowe, who were both appearing at the Prince's Theatre, Bradford. After a few weeks the family moved on to the next show in another town, somewhat fulfilling the saying 'The show must go on'.

West began learning his stagecraft at an early age, working in repertory before achieving success on the London stage, notably in West End productions. His list of impressive stage credits include *King Lear, Richard II, Edward II, A Month in the Country, A Room with a View, Henry IV, The Clandestine Marriage, Death of a Salesman, Macbeth, The Birthday Party*, and many others.

He has starred in many television productions, including *Edward VII, Horatio Bottomley, Crime and Punishment, Murder Most Horrid, Good Night Sweetheart*, and has portrayed Winston Churchill three times (*Hiroshima*, 1995; *The Last Bastion*, 1984; and *Churchill and His Generals*, 1979).

He has also portrayed sundry sirs, lords, judges, overseers, superintendents, doctors, high-ranking military officers, and in two animated feature cartoon series, he was the voice of King Otto (*The Big Knights*, 1999) and King Hrothgar (*Beowulf*, 1998).

His motion picture credits include *Nicholas and Alexandra, The Day of the Jackal, Oliver Twist, Hedda, Agatha, The Thirty-nine Steps, Cry Freedom, Joan of Arc* and *Villa des roses*.

In 1965 he married the equally well-known star Prunella Scales. In 1984 he was awarded a CBE for his services to the profession. Although he only spent the first three months of his life in Bradford, he visits the city professionally from time to time. There is a glint in his eye when he says he is proud of his northern roots – and he loves Bradford.

Sir Mortimer Wheeler CH, MC
Archaeologist

From roaming on Baildon moors picking up pottery and following an archaeological interest inherited from his father, the young boy from Saltaire was to become one of the most notable archaeologists of the twentieth century.

Mortimer (Rick) Wheeler was born in Glasgow in 1890. When he was four his family moved to live in Moorhead Lane, Saltaire, where his father took the post of chief leader writer of the *Bradford Observer*. He was at Bradford Grammar School from the age of nine to sixteen, and it was on the moors in Baildon where his interest in archaeology was kindled, collecting Roman pottery and making a study of the cup and ring marks.

While at Bradford Grammar School it seems he could have flourished either as a writer or an artist. He produced a private journal and had one of his oil paintings hung in the Bradford spring exhibition. In the end his ambitions to become an artist evaporated, but not before he had made a modest reputation as a cartoonist.

When his family moved to London in 1906 he began his studies at London University. During the First World War he distinguished himself as an officer with the Royal Field Artillery, winning the Military Cross and being mentioned in dispatches. After the war he was appointed to the National Museum of Wales, and in 1926 became keeper of the London Museum, until service during the Second World War.

Between the wars Mortimer Wheeler had taken over work already begun at the Roman fort at Segontium near Caernarvon, and had excavated the Roman fort at Brecon. At Maiden Castle, where weapons and skeletons were discovered, he reconstructed the battle by which the Romans overcame the defenders. His excavations at Verulamium, or St Albans, the oldest Roman city in Britain, shed further new light on Roman England. He also worked in Brittany, Normandy, India, Pakistan and throughout Asia. Later he toured the world lecturing, and collecting many distinguished honours. In 1952 he was knighted, and he became a Companion of Honour in 1967.

It was Sir Mortimer Wheeler and his colleagues who brought archaeology into the living room with the popular television programme *Animal, Vegetable, Mineral?* in which historical items were discussed and panellists had to guess their origin.

The 6ft 3in Sir Mortimer with his ample moustache looked ever the distinguished gentleman he was. He was voted TV Personality of the Year in 1954.

Sir Mortimer Wheeler died on 22 July 1976 aged eighty-six.

Billie Whitelaw CBE

Actress

Billie Whitelaw is regarded as the greatest interpreter of the plays of Samuel Beckett.

Born on 6 June 1932 in Coventry of Liverpudlian parents, she came to Bradford during the war when she was nine, having been sent originally to relatives in Liverpool to escape the Coventry bombing, only to find that Liverpool was being bombed too.

Billie arrived in Bradford to join her father, whose firm, GEC, had been evacuated there. Her mother soon joined them at the new family home, 3 Ruskin Avenue, on the Haworth Road estate. Billie attended Daisy Hill Primary School, Thornton Grammar School and then Grange High School and the City High School for Girls. With the sudden death of her father her mother worked at Sharpe's to supplement her widow's pension. During this time that Billie took over the running of the house: shopping, cleaning, and making meals for her mother's return from work.

It was developing a stutter that led Billie into an acting career. Her mother thought that amateur theatricals might help her conquer it. In 1943 she enrolled at the Bradford Playhouse, then run by Esmé Church and J.B. Priestley. Soon she was spotted by a BBC producer to play little boys on the radio.

By the time she was fifteen her voice had been heard on the wireless over one hundred times. She left school and mixed work in the theatre with stints behind the counter at Busby's department store on Manningham Lane, in the lingerie and toy departments.

In 1950 she landed a role in the eight-part BBC TV dramatisation of *The Secret Garden*. Aged nineteen she joined the cast of Penguin Players, making her stage debut at the Keighley Hippodrome in their production of *His Excellency* (1952).

Billie made her big-screen debut in *The Fake* (1953), and went on to co-star with Peter Finch in *No Love for Johnnie* (1960). In 1967 she won a British Academy Best Actress Award for her role in Albert Finney's *Charlie Bubbles*. She has since turned in highly effective movie performances. A particularly memorable role was that of the ill-fated nanny in the 1976 film *The Omen*. Other notable films were *The Krays* (1990), in which she played the mother of the British gangsters; the housekeeper in Franco Zeffirelli's version of Charlotte Brontë's *Jane Eyre* (1996); and the blind laundress in *Quills* (2000).

On stage her interpretation of the work of Samuel Beckett has been highly praised. In 1980 she was made an honorary doctor of letters at Bradford University. In 1991 she was awarded the CBE in the Queen's Birthday Honours List.

Richard Whiteley

Television Personality

Richard Whiteley has endeared himself to millions as the charismatic presenter of Channel 4's longest running hit *Countdown*; his was also the first face ever seen on Channel 4.

Richard was born on 28 December 1943, the family living at Ferncliffe Drive, Baildon. He attended the local kindergarten in Baildon, then Heather Bank Prep School. The family business, Thomas Whiteley & Co., worsted manufacturers, was based in Eccleshill. Richard attended the Methodist Chapel in Baildon and joined the Wesleyan Methodist Cub Pack.

In 1957, aged thirteen, he was sent to Giggleswick, the school his father had attended. In 1962 he was offered a place to read English at Christ's College, Cambridge. To fill in time before the move he taught at a primary school in Bingley, and drove a delivery van for the local grocer.

Leaving Christ's College in 1965 he joined Independent Television News as an editorial trainee, and three years later joined the newly formed Yorkshire Television as an assistant producer and reporter. Austin Mitchell, who had recently returned from working in New Zealand, also joined Yorkshire Television and together they formed the well-known Yorkshire duo on *Calendar*.

In all, over twenty-seven years, Richard made over 10,000 appearances for YTV's news magazine *Calendar*. He is also a versatile interviewer, at home in both serious and light-hearted mode. In 1982 he branched out in a different direction as the host of Channel 4's new quiz programme *Countdown*, which is still a massive hit.

He also presented a chat show where he did not know who the guests were going to be, quite a feat when as a rule presenters have information collected by a researcher so that they never 'dry up'. He has made guest appearances on other TV shows, including *Mrs Merton, Have I Got News for You, This is Your Life* and *Songs of Praise*.

Richard has vast experience of live presentations and chairing television debates. He is regarded by many politicians and business people as a well-informed, likeable, but incisive interviewer. He has interviewed every prime minister since Harold Macmillan, and holds the honorary position of Mayor of Wetwang, a small village in the East Riding of Yorkshire.

George Whyte-Watson

Pioneer in the Treatment of Cancer

'We don't talk of a cure, we talk of the survival rate; not only that, but also the quality of survival. Ours was a new approach, the first real change in treatment for fifty years, and it seems to be standing up as the years go on.'

Born in 1908, George Whyte-Watson came to Bradford after holding a house position at the Edinburgh Royal Infirmary in 1932, being appointed Deputy to the Superintendent at St Luke's Hospital. He was made a consultant in 1939.

In 1946 he joined the staff of the Bradford Royal Infirmary, as Senior Consultant Surgeon at hospitals in the Bradford area, but is perhaps best known for the breakthrough in the treatment of breast cancer with his colleague Professor Turner.

Working in their spare time Mr Whyte-Watson and Dr Turner, Consultant Pathologist at Bradford Royal Infirmary, discovered a new treatment for breast cancer, which at the time was described as an 'outstanding medical achievement'. Their discovery was applied first to patients in the advanced stages of the disease, and they gradually started applying chemotherapy as a primary treatment in breast cancer.

Tracing the disease in its early stages was important, and George Whyte-Watson was instrumental in getting self-examination added to procedures already carried out at clinics. Malignant tumours of the breast were usually painless and only found accidentally, so this superficial examination was worthwhile, as most swellings of the breast, especially in young women, were benign.

Mr Whyte-Watson retired in 1973 but still continued research into breast cancer. The legacy he left in Bradford are the untold hundreds of women who are still alive today due to his relentless pioneering work.

He was a former Chairman of the Bradford Division of the British Medical Association and a Director of Bradford Park Avenue Football Club.

Within a few months of retiring Mr Whyte-Watson died the day before his sixty-fifth birthday in 1974.

There is a memorial plaque in Bradford Cathedral commemorating Mr Whyte-Watson's life.

Maurice Wilson MC

Adventurer and Everest Mountaineer

Maurice Wilson was truly a remarkable man who, were it not for an untimely death, would probably be remembered as one of the city's greatest adventurers.

He was born on 21 April 1898 and lived in Cecil Avenue, Little Horton. Maurice was the son of Mark Wilson, principal of the piece goods manufacturers Holme Top Mills, also in Little Horton.

After attending Carlton Street High School, Maurice spent his early years in the textile industry until his service in the First World War. In 1918 at the age of twenty as an Infantry Officer with the 3rd/6th West Yorkshire Regiment serving in France, he charged a German machine-gun crew single-handed, put them out of action, and returned with the gun. He was awarded the Military Cross for his actions.

On demobilisation he was employed in the Bradford stuff trade with the firm of Mason & Dutton, but later went to New Zealand and established a ladies' gown business in Wellington. In 1932, no longer being active in business, he returned to England and took up flying as a hobby, gaining his pilot's licence, which included parachute descents, and it was at this time that he had the idea of attempting to reach the summit of Mount Everest. Though he had no experience of long-distance flying, he got his plane to India, and eventually to his base on the India–Nepal border, but there his luck deserted him. Permission to fly over the border was refused so he sold the aeroplane and disappeared.

In great secrecy Wilson attempted to tackle Everest on foot, managing to persuade three Sherpas to go with him. On 25 March 1934 the little party left Darjeeling secretly with Wilson dressed as a Tibetan porter. No more was heard until four months later on 7 July when the Sherpas reappeared to tell an astonishing story. With Wilson they had made the journey to the foot of Everest in twenty-five days, over some of the most difficult terrain in the world.

Following the route of the 1933 expedition, they reached Camp II at 19,000 feet and remained for two weeks under terrible conditions, until the weather drove them back down the valley. They tried again and this time reached Camp III at 21,000 feet. It was here that the Sherpas realised that a further climb up the ice-covered North Col was impossible and refused to go on. On 23 May with intrepid determination Wilson set off alone carrying three loaves of bread, two tins of porridge, a light tent and a camera. He was never seen alive again. In 1935 a reconnaissance party led by the famous Eric Shipton found Wilson's body 300 yards above Camp III. He must have died in his sleep from exhaustion as he still had plenty of food left. They buried him in a deep crevasse in North Col.

Wilson's diary was complete up to the time of his death. The last entry reads: 'Off again; gorgeous day.'

Tom Winnard

Bradford Northern and Great Britain Rugby Player

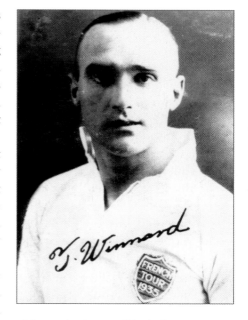

Tom Winnard, captain of Bradford Northern, was one of the most brilliant and spectacular three-quarters in rugby league, backing up his try-scoring feats by his ability to kick goals. It was often said that he had won a match on his own and he was the first player ever to kick a goal at Odsal Stadium when the club played their first match against Huddersfield in 1934.

Born in Wigan on 6 January 1910, Tom was not an academic schoolboy. He spent most of his early years helping his father run a greengrocery market stall in their home town. However, whatever he lacked in academic knowledge he certainly proved himself at St Patrick's School Wigan, where many future rugby league stars had their debuts.

His first team of note was St Helen's, where he made a name for himself in the League and Lancashire Championship cup matches. This had many clubs chasing him including Bradford Northern (then playing at Birch Lane, West Bowling) who signed him in 1933 for a club record fee of £385, thus sidestepping Wigan and Halifax who were also keen to sign him.

Throughout his many seasons with Northern, he always gave 100 per cent performances, which brought out the best in his teammates. As well as his ability to set up play, he was a superb try and goal scorer in his own right. He was the first Northern player to kick 6 goals in one match (against Featherstone in 1934 at the new Odsal Stadium).

In 1935 he was selected to play in the Rugby League Tour of France, and won his first cap in 1937 playing for Great Britain against France in Halifax.

His best season was 1936/7 when he kicked 87 goals and scored 22 tries for a personal tally of 240 points, making him the first Bradford player to break through the 200 points barrier in any one season, setting a new club points scoring record. Among his many records the most extraordinary was scoring four hat-tricks on Christmas Day in 1936, 1937, 1939 and 1943, perhaps not even surpassed to date.

With the advent of the Second World War and restricted games, he made only two appearances in the season 1941/2, none in 1942 and only eight in 1943, before finally retiring on 1 January 1944. He then joined the Green Howards and saw active service in Sicily and Italy.

In 1945 he was demobbed and lived with his family in Wyke. During the next few years he was a school caretaker at Edmund Campion School, Tong.

Tom Winnard died after a short illness in 1988 aged seventy-eight, a well-respected former Bradford Northern stalwart.

Humbert Wolfe CB, CBE

Poet and Civil Servant

Wolfe's poetry has been described as expressing a 'Chopinesque wistfulness of the heart'.

He was born Umberto Wolfe in Milan, Italy, on 5 January 1885. The family moved to Bradford when he was just a few months old and he spent the first seventeen years of his life here. His father Martin was a member of the Bradford wool trade, and the family home was at Mount Royd, off Manningham Lane.

After attending a preparatory school he went to Bradford Grammar School, aged seven, where his interest in poetry became evident. His first published effort was a crib on Milton's 'Lycidas', offering a farewell to the steam trams which were at that time giving way to their electric successors. The poem was published in *The Bradfordian* and others followed.

Wolfe was at Wadham College for four years and during this time he began to widen his interests. Politics came as much into the picture as poetry, and that, no doubt, determined him to join the Civil Service in 1908. He entered the Board of Trade and played a part in the formation of a Labour Department. This led to the beginning of the Ministry of Labour, where his unusual personality, solidity and brilliance of mind soon brought him to the fore. From 1912 to 1915 he was among the band of able Civil Servants who, with Sir William Beveridge, organised labour exchanges and unemployment insurance schemes.

In 1915 he was transferred to the newly formed Ministry of Munitions as controller of labour regulations, serving under Lloyd George and Winston Churchill. In 1918 he was awarded a CBE; the Companion of the Order of Bath followed in 1925. During these years he was still writing poetry, averaging two volumes of verse a year. He also found time for much reviewing and prose writing on a larger scale. He turned his hand with success to biography, writing a life of Shelley and portraits of Tennyson and George Moore.

In 1934 he became head of the old Department of Employment and Training and in March 1938 Deputy Secretary to the Minister for Employment. As war loomed, the problem of manpower became increasingly urgent. In January 1939 the call was made for the recruitment of men and women for national services. Wolfe's experience was of the utmost value, and six months after the opening of the campaign a million people for Civil Defence, the Territorial Amy and the Auxiliary Fire Service were recruited. When the official National Service handbook had been distributed all over the country, Wolfe said at a private dinner that he was the only living author whose first edition ran to 20 million copies!

All this was at the cost of his life, working sixteen hours a day and suffering from high blood pressure, and with full knowledge of the consequences. He died in London at his home in Mount Street, Mayfair, on 5 January 1940, his fifty-fifth birthday.

Joseph Wright

Editor of the English Dialect Dictionary

Few famous men have had such an un-promising start in life as Joseph Wright: his childhood was one of unrelieved poverty. He never had the benefit of orthodox schooling and could neither read nor write until he was seventeen, yet such was the quality of his character that he managed almost single-handedly to edit and organise the publication of the six-volume *English Dialect Dictionary*.

Born at Park Hill Farm Cottage, Thackley, in a tiny one-roomed house on 31 October 1855, Joseph was the son of humble parents. His father took the family to Eston near Middlesbrough, but eventually Mrs Wright left her husband there, returned home, and went with her three little boys to the Clayton workhouse. Mrs Wright later left the workhouse with her family and set up home in a one-roomed cottage in Town Lane, Idle. Other moves took place and it was to the 'Spite and Malice House', a one-roomed cottage in Woodend, that his father returned, and subsequently died.

At the age of six Joseph began to earn his living by taking quarrymen's tools to be sharpened by a local blacksmith, a year later becoming a doffer, working half-time at Saltaire Mills earning 3s 6d a week. When he left school, reading and writing were still as remote to him as any of the sciences, and he spoke only with the broadest of Yorkshire dialects.

At fifteen he became a fully fledged wool sorter and was able to establish his mother and family in reasonable comfort at 6 Wellington Street, Woodend, Windhill. The family attended the Primitive Methodist Church, though later Joseph joined the Church of England. Some time in 1868 he left Saltaire Mill and went to work at Stephen Wildman's mill (known as Baildon Bridge Mill) situated between Shipley and Baildon, and now earned 9s a week.

On hearing his fellow workmen reading aloud news about the Franco-Prussian War in 1870, he became determined to learn to read and write, a task he accom-plished with the aid of a copy of *Pilgrim's Progress* and the Bible. He began to study French and German and went to evening classes for mathematics at the Bradford Mechanics' Institute, a walk of three miles each way per session.

In 1876, having saved £40, Wright went for a term to Heidelberg University. On his return he taught at Springfield House (sometimes referred as Watson's Academy) off Manningham Lane. In 1885 he proceeded again to Heidelberg where he took up teaching and was awarded a doctorate of philosophy, a remarkable feat for someone who fifteen years earlier had been illiterate! In 1888 Wright returned to England to accept a lecturing position at Oxford, teaching German composition and history. Shortly afterwards the Taylorian Institute created a post for him, a lectureship in Teutonic philology, thus giving him a real start in academic life. He was later appointed Deputy Professor of Philology and was then elected a full professor in succession to Max Muller.

His *A Grammar of the Dialect of Windhill in the West Riding of Yorkshire* appeared in 1892, but his major work was the *English Dialect Dictionary*. He took on over two million slips of paper containing dialect words and phrases from William Skeat who had started the dictionary in 1873 at the request of the English Dialect Society. The slips of paper weighed almost 2 tons, whose result, when he had finished adding and subtracting, was the six-volume dictionary which bears his name.

No publisher could be found so he spent £2,000 of his own money on the project. Just as the money was running out, in stepped the future prime minister, A.J. Balfour (then at the Treasury), who managed to secure £200 a year for three years to help Wright complete the work. The first volume came out in 1896, and by 1905 the task was complete. The dictionary contains about 100,000 words, illustrated by some 500,000 quotations.

During the following years many honours were bestowed on the professor. These included degrees from the universities of Dublin, Aberdeen, Leeds and Oxford, and a fellowship from the British Academy. He was also a fellow of several colleges at Oxford and Cambridge, and received many honorary degrees from several other universities. He was Vice-President of the Royal Society of Literature.

The six volumes continue to be of immense value to scholars of varieties of English. Nothing of comparable breadth or depth of dialect scholarship has been published in Britain since – a truly remarkable feat by a young, illiterate, workhouse boy from Thackley.

After a short illness Joseph Wright died at his home in Oxford on 27 February 1930 aged seventy-four and was buried at Wolvercote Cemetery.

Acknowledgements

To the many people who have contributed in some way to make this book possible – thank you all.

Margaret Wood, who for the last three years has given me her utmost support, and especially for improving my original script and typing it up. I thank her for her research, her patience and her support. Without her this book would never have been completed.

Bob Duckett, ex-Bradford Libraries, for his support and enthusiasm. From the beginning Bob, like me, saw the need for this type of book about Bradford's heritage. I would also like to thank him for his kindness in sub-editing the original manuscript.

Carl Gresham – the friend of the stars, whose help made it possible for me to contact many stars of screen, theatre and TV, with introductions to them and their agents, and for the photograph of Kiki Dee.

The staff at Bradford Reference Library for their help and support on my many visits for research. Special thanks to Susan Caton, Trevor Scott, Peter Walker, Carol Greenwood and Mick Birdsall, for whom nothing was too much trouble – thank you all.

Mohammed Ajeeb for an interesting interview, biography and a photograph. *Bob Appleyard* for the interview and personal photograph. *Tasmin Archer* for pleasant interviews and a personal photograph. *Philippa Bambech*, daughter of Richard Eurich, for photographs of and information about both her father Richard and her grandfather Frederick Eurich. *Lee Birkinshaw*, of the *T&A*, for help in collating photographs. *Pam Boyd*, Regimental Headquarters, The Prince of Wales's Own Regiment of Yorkshire, 3 Tower Street, York, Regimental Museum West Yorks (Bradford Pals), for kind permission to use photographs of Eric Anderson, Samuel Meekosha and George Chafer, all VC recipients. At *Bradford Grammar School*, Mrs S. South, Librarian, and Katie Harrison, Assistant Librarian, for their help with information on former pupils. *Bradford Libraries*, for permission to use photographs of Sir Titus Salt, Frederick Delius, Samuel Lister, Margaret McMillan, Halliwell Sutcliffe and W.E. Forster. *John Briggs* for an interview, biography and a personal photograph. *Sue Buck* for an interview and personal photograph of her sister, the late Barbara Jane Harrison, George Cross recipient. *Debbie Cain and family* for photographs and information on her grandfather Albert Modley. *Garth Cawood* for the pleasant interview with a showbusiness colleague, and photograph. *Brian Close* for a frank interview. *David Coates*, Managing Director of Newsquest Bradford, and *Perry Austin-Clarke*, Editor of the *Telegraph & Argus*, for their kind permission to use the photographs of: Sir Edward Appleton, David Bairstow,

Rodney Bewes, Dickie Bond, Barbara Castle, Brian Close, Ian Clough, Harry Corbett, Bob Cryer, Andrea Dunbar, Richard Dunn, Vic Feather, Gareth Gates, David Hockney, Joe Johnson, Francis Laidler, Jim Laker, Bertram Priestman, Tony Richardson, William Rothenstein (painting), Leslie Sands, Harvey Smith, Robert Turner, Tomothy West, Sir Mortimer Wheeler, Billie Whitelaw and Maurice Wilson. *Richard Coatesworth* for his help with the computer programming. *Beverley Cole*, National Railway Museum, York, for her help with the biography of Frank Newbould and his photograph from the collection. *John Culme* for information on Marie Studholme. *John Damman* of Bradford Hospitals NHS Trust, for permission to use part of the text on Professor Robert Turner and George Whyte-Watson from *The History of Bradford Hospitals from 1780*. *Reuben Davison*: many thanks for his help in the collation and scanning of new photographs. *Kiki Dee* for an in-depth interview with my friend and colleague. *John Duttine* for an interview and personal photograph by Peter Rodgers of Padstow. *Adrian Edmondson* for an interview and information about his career and early life in Bradford, and *Beaj Johnson*, photographer, for kind permission to use his portrait. *John Fisher and staff* at the libraries and Guildhall Art Gallery, Corporation of London, for additional information on and photograph of Sir Guy Bracewell Smith. *Trevor Foster* for a pleasant interview and personal photograph. *Harry Gration* for the biography of his early life in Bradford and a personal photograph. *Steven Hartley* for an agreeable interview and a personal photograph. *Lord Healey of Riddlesden* for permission to use some text from his autobiography *My Secret Planet*, additional information and a personal photograph. *Graham Herrington* of Oak Lane Studios for additional local photographs. *Miss Joan Hoyle* for additional information on and a photograph of her late brother, Sir Fred Hoyle. *International Artistes of London* – Agents Michele Millburn and Sarah Coward: many thanks for information on and a photograph of Peter Firth. *Anthony Jeffries* and family for information on and a photograph of the late David Jeffries. *Councillor J.S. King* for the foreword to this book. He has a broad local knowledge and is an authority on Bradford's heritage. *Ken Kitson* for the story of his early life in Bradford and a personal photograph. *Michael Koch-Osborne* for the history of his forebears, William and Benjamin Jowett, and family photographs. *Martin Lampkin* for information about his son Dougie and a photograph. *Keith Laybourn* for additional information on Philip Snowden, and *Graham Hall* for his photograph. *George Layton* for an interview and a personal photograph. *David Lee* for information on his early life in Bradford and his showbusiness career, and a photograph. *Father L. Lister* for permission to use the photograph of Msgr J. O'Connor (Father Brown) (St Cuthbert's RC Church, Bradford). *Yvonne McGregor* for details of her early life and a personal photograph. *James Magennis* for the photograph of his late father, James Magennis VC. *Shahid Malik and Lisa* for a very interesting interview, biography and a personal photograph. *Peter Maufe* for the photograph of his late father, Thomas H.B. Maufe VC. *Joe Mercer* for the photographs of himself and his late brother Manny. *Austin Mitchell* for an interesting interview, biography and a photograph. *Adrian Moorhouse* for the information on his early life and a personal photograph. *Sir Ken Morrison* for information about his early life in Bradford and a personal photograph. *Mrs N. Mosley* for additional information on and photograph of her late husband Bryan being awarded an honorary MA at Bradford University in 1995. *Chris Owen* of Ulverston for his help and additional information on the Bradford wrestlers Dennis Mitchell, Jim Breaks and Les Kellett, and photographs from his private collection. *Doug Padgett* for an interview, a personal biography and a photograph. *Edward Peel* for the story of his early years in Bradford and a personal photograph. *Doreen Petherbridge* for a photograph of her brother-in-law Edward Petherbridge. *Mark Pharaoh*, Curator of the Mawson Antarctic Collection, Adelaide University, for information about and a photograph of Sir Douglas Mawson. *Duncan Preston* for information about his early life in Bradford and a photograph. *Mike Priestley* for an interview, personal biography and photograph. *David Roper* for information on his early life and a personal photograph. *Simon Rouse* for a very interesting interview about his early life in Bradford and a personal photograph. *The curator and staff of the Royal Fusiliers Museum*, Tower of London, for permission to use the photograph of Matthew Hughes VC. *Walter Scott*, Printers, for permission to use the photograph of Bishop Blunt. *Jim Sewell*, City Archivist, Corporation of London Records Office, for additional information on Sir Guy Bracewell Smith. *Roger Shackleton* for the photograph of his late father Len Shackleton. *Mrs Silver* for information and a personal photograph of her late husband Jonathan. *David Stone* for the photograph of John Coates from his private collection. *Mollie Sugden* for a delightful interview and personal photograph. *Steven Tempest-Mitchell* for information about and photograph of his late father Dennis Mitchell. *Darren Thomas* for his kindness in supplying the photographs of Michael Rennie and James Douglas Hill from the Kobal Collection Ltd. *Stephanie Turner* for her biography and a personal photograph. *Timothy West* for a pleasant interview. *Richard Whiteley* for information on his early life, a photograph and permission to use extracts from his autobiography *Himoff!* (Orion, 2000).

Every effort has been made to contact organisations and individuals regarding the reproduction of photographs, images and text included in this book. The material has been used in good faith and the author regrets any omissions or misrepresentations, but does not accept liability, irrespective of how these may have arisen.

Derek A.J. Lister
Bingley 2004

About the Author

Soldier, Author and Explorer of Kwa Zululand

Derek Lister was born on 2 May 1938 at Walden Drive, Heaton, Bradford. The family moved to 30 Legrams Street, a small back-to-back house in Listerhills in the summer of 1939. He attended St Patrick's Nursery and Junior School, Westgate, and later their secondary modern school (affectionately known as White Abbey College).

He left school in 1953 aged fifteen and was employed at Brown Muffs department store in the gents tailoring department – highlights of his time there included selling Bishop Blunt a Pacamac, and a pair of trousers to one of the famous Dambusters. In 1954 he met his heroes Laurel and Hardy at the Midland Hotel when he was a cheeky sixteen-year-old, knocking on their hotel room door and asking for their autograph. He was invited in, and enjoyed a cool drink in the company of the two icons and their wives – a moment to treasure. Derek left Brown Muffs in 1955 to join Burton's Tailoring in Westgate and then did his National Service in 1956. He signed on as a regular soldier and saw active service in Aden.

Back in civvy street Derek worked for a while at Grattan's Warehouse, then Stenhouse Insurance Brokers in Well Street. During this time he had a rock'n'roll group called Dal Stevens and the Four Dukes, and for five years worked as a semi-professional disc-jockey at the Gaumont and Majestic ballrooms in Bradford (see his *Bradford's Rock'n'Roll: The Golden Years 1959–1965*, Bradford Libraries, 1991).

In 1965 he embarked on a career in selling and sold insurance, advertising (for the *Bradford Pictorial*), trolls, prams and, until 1969 when he joined Concord Lighting, working in Yorkshire and the north-east. After being made redundant in 1980 he joined the leisure industry, selling and later marketing equipment to sports and leisure centres. He retired in 2003.

His hobbies include writing, training at the gym, metal detecting and collecting medals. He is a member of the Orders Medals Research Society and an authority on British campaign medals. He visits South Africa annually, primarily Kwa Zululand where he explores the areas involved in the Zulu Wars of 1877–9. The highlight of these trips? Contracting tic fever.